"Stop! Don't learn another sign until you've read Michelle Jay's *A Student's Guide to Mastering ASL Grammar*! Clear, easy to understand, and loaded with excellent examples this book is one that every ASL student and teacher ought to keep "*handy*!""

William G. Vicars, Ed.D.
Associate Professor of ASL and Deaf Studies
California State University, Sacramento
(Also known as "Dr. Bill" of **www.lifeprint.com**)

"Think you can't learn American Sign Language? Well, think again. Start ASL's book, *A Student's Guide to Mastering ASL Grammar* makes learning ASL grammar and syntax not only fun but easy to understand. This guide gives you the tools you need to feel comfortable communicating in the Deaf community."

Pearl Feder, L.C.S.W., Editor & Coordinator
SayWhatClub Social Media
www.saywhatclub.com

"There is so much more to signing than just learning the hand shapes and movements. ASL is all about its own syntax, phonology and grammar. This book does a great job of exploring what makes ASL its own unique language. Start ASL has done it again!"

John Miller, Co-Founder, Educator
www.signingsavvy.com

"I found this book to be valuable as a quick reference for non-vocabulary aspects of ASL. I recommend this book to anyone who needs to master ASL as a second language."

Omer Zak, Owner
DEAF-INFO
www.zak.co.il/deaf-info

"Studying ASL Linguistics at Gallaudet University was truly an eye opening experience, even for me, a Deaf person, who has already mastered American Sign Language since childhood. Combining all of the grammatical aspects of ASL to form a complete idea is not easy for the beginning signer. Luckily, *A Student's Guide to Mastering ASL Grammar* explains all of this, how to execute, and then some! Great job to Michelle Jay for making this available and so clearly for the new and not-so-new signer!"

MJ Williams, Author & Website Creator/Owner
www.babiesandsignlanguage.com

"As an ASL instructor for high school students, I am always looking for ways to improve my students' understanding of ASL structure. *A Student's Guide to Mastering ASL Grammar* is a great tool for beginning ASL students to use along with class instruction for understanding the grammatical and conceptual nature of ASL. The book is very user friendly and structured well."

Cindy Dawes, ASL Instructor
Fivay High School

Don't Just "Sign"... COMMUNICATE!

A Student's Guide to Mastering ASL Grammar

by Michelle Jay

Judea Media, LLC—Los Angeles, CA

2011

Inquiries should be addressed to:
Judea Media, LLC
publish@judeamedia.com

The publisher and author disclaim any personal liability, directly or indirectly, for advice or information presented within. Although the author and publisher have prepared this manuscript with utmost care and diligence and have made every effort to ensure the accuracy and completeness of the information contained within, we assume no responsibility for errors, inaccuracies, omissions or inconsistencies.

Publisher's Cataloging-in-Publication

Jay, Michelle.

    Don't just "sign" ... communicate! : a student's guide to mastering ASL grammar / by Michelle Jay.
    p. cm.
    Includes bibliographical references and index.
    ISBN-13 978-0-9845294-4-5
    ISBN-10 0-9845294-4-6
    Library of Congress Control Number: 2011902570

    1. American Sign Language—Study and teaching. 2. American Sign Language—Handbooks manuals, etc. 3. Deaf—Means of communication. I. Jay, Michelle. II. Title.

HV2474.J39 2011

419 J39 dja   2011902570

Printed and bound in the United States of America.

Contents

American Sign Language Grammar • 57

American Sign Language Phonology • 59

American Sign Language Morphology • 71

American Sign Language Syntax • 89

Introduction

It wasn't until 1960 that American Sign Language was recognized as a real language with its own grammar and syntax. American Sign Language is its own language, completely separate from English. Like any other language, ASL has its own rules of phonology, morphology, and syntax.

What you may find difficult when first learning American Sign Language is figuring out ASL grammar and how it is different from English. This is important because if you don't know ASL grammar, you aren't signing ASL. While signing, it can be easy to slip into using English word order and grammar if you aren't fully aware of ASL structure.

To help with this issue, I have created this book which contains all the essentials of ASL grammar in a format that is easy to follow, understand, and study. This book doesn't use any special activities or beat-around-the-bush learning techniques. It just outlines the most important parts of ASL grammar that you need to know.

The best way to learn the grammar of any language is to converse with the native users of that language. However, many ASL students, particularly hearing students, have difficulty picking up ASL grammar from conversation alone. This book is essential for any ASL student who wants to learn how to accurately sign in ASL. After you have finished this book, you will be fully armed with the right information to improve your skills and move toward fluency in American Sign Language.

So, let's get started!

How to Use This Book

In this section:

- **Understanding the Main Topics**
- **Useful Tools**
- **Who Should Use This Book**

Understanding the Main Topics

This book consists of six main sections that each focus on one part of ASL grammar:

Introduction to American Sign Language
This section explains some basic ASL background information and how to make sure you are learning ASL and not a signing system.

ASL Signs and Vocabulary
This section outlines important vocabulary concepts that aren't explained in most ASL dictionaries.

ASL Grammar
This is a short section that will prepare you for the ASL grammar rule sections.

ASL Phonology
This section explains the rules of ASL phonology and how signs are formed.

ASL Morphology
This section explains the rules of ASL morphology and how signs are inflected to create meaning.

ASL Syntax
This section explains the rules of ASL syntax and how to form correct sentences in ASL.

I recommend reading the book once over before studying in detail. This will help if you have difficulty understanding something that is actually mentioned later in the book.

Understanding these sections and knowing how they relate to each other, and ASL grammar in general, will help you get the most out of this book.

Useful Tools

Introduction to Glossing

Because ASL is an unwritten language, glossing is a technique used to create a written version of ASL. In this book, I will gloss ASL sentences the best I can to give examples of how to use ASL grammar when signing.

The examples I use in this book tend to be of shorter ASL sentences because this book is meant to focus on certain parts of ASL grammar. Once you understand each part of ASL grammar, you will be able to construct more complicated sentences on your own as you involve yourself in the Deaf community and apply the grammar rules in actual conversations.

Glossing is not difficult to understand, but it is necessary for me to provide a short lesson so you are able to follow the examples in this book.

When glossing a sentence in ASL, I will use the following rules:

Every sign is written in CAPITAL LETTERS.

ME LIKE RICE
"I like rice."

Signs that are translated into more than one English word are shown with dashes. The lowercase words are implied, so they do not need to be signed separately.

YESTERDAY MOM GO-to STORE
"Mom went to the store yesterday."

TWO-OF-US WATCH MOVIE FINISH
"We watched a movie."

Fingerspelling is shown with dashes between the capital letters or with "fs-".

HER NAME S-U-Z-Y
HER NAME fs-SUZY
"Her name is Suzy."

Lexicalized fingerspelling is shown with a number sign ("#"). When you see the number sign, this means you fingerspell the word, but use the lexicalized version that is produced more like a sign than like a fingerspelled word.

SHE ARRIVE #EARLY
"She arrived early."

Signs that are repeated are shown with plus symbols ("+"). The number of symbols indicates the number of times the sign is repeated.

Signs that are stressed (inflected) are shown in italics.

SPEECH *LONG BORING CONTINUE+++*
"That long boring speech seemed to last forever!"

A sign signed with both hands is indicated with (2h), signed with your dominant hand (dh), and signed with your non-dominant hand (nh).

Classifiers are indicated with "CL". The classifier handshape is after the colon and what the classifier is representing is in parenthesis.

Quotes after a sign specify how the sign is inflected (if necessary).

(2h)CL:4(people in line)"long line"
"That line is so long!"

Signs between pronouns indicate directionality. The words indicate the direction of the sign between referents.

he-GIVE-her BOOK
"He gave her the book."

Non-Manual markers and facial expressions are shown on a line above the gloss. For example, the sentence below tells you to have a "wh-word question" facial expression when signing WHERE.

       ____whq
YOU GO WHERE?
"Where did you go?"

Other non-manual markers are shown with the following:

Topicalization: __t
Yes/no question: __y/n
Rhetorical question: __rhq
Conditional statement: __cond

Affirmative statement: __aff
Negative statement: __neg
Mouth movement: __"_"

For example:

      _whq
HE/SHE WHO?
"Who is he/she?"

_____y/n
DEAF YOU?
"Are you Deaf?"

      __rhq _____neg
ME HUNGRY, WHY? EAT LUNCH NOT
"I'm hungry because I didn't eat lunch."

_____cond _____aff
TODAY RAIN, GAME CANCEL
"If it rains today, the game will be cancelled."

_____t _whq
THAT GIRL, WHO?
"Who is that girl?"

_____t _____aff
MY DAD, THAT MAN
"That man is my dad."

      _"cha"
ME WANT LARGE SODA
"I want a very large soda."

You will learn more about these non-manual markers and sentence types in a later section.

Pictures and Images

In this book, I use pictures to explain some vocabulary and concepts. The arrows in the pictures indicate the movement of the sign and the pictures are always from your perspective (as if you are facing me while I sign). However, I know that learning signs from pictures can be difficult, so I highly recommend using an ASL dictionary and looking up the words you don't understand.

I also do not explain or illustrate all the signs I mention, so I recommend having a dictionary handy in case I mention a sign you don't already know.

Glossary

You can use the glossary that is provided in the back of this book if you come across a word that you don't understand.

Translation Study Sheet

In the back of the book, you will find a translation study sheet that provides English versus ASL sentence examples for most of the different topics covered in this book. If you ever need to look up an example of a grammar rule covered in the book, this is the place to look.

Who Should Use This Book

If you are learning or are interested in learning American Sign Language, then this book is for you. It doesn't matter why you are learning ASL—this information is necessary for all ASL students and anyone who plans to use ASL. This book will teach you the differences between ASL and English and how to sign accurately in American Sign Language.

1 Introduction to **American Sign Language**

In this section:

- **Make Sure You Are Learning ASL**

In 1989 American Sign Language was finally recognized as a standard language by the U.S. Supreme Court. They recognized ASL as having its own grammar, syntax, vocabulary, and culture. ASL was then able to be offered in schools to satisfy foreign language requirements.

Since then, there has been a huge increase in ASL popularity. According to a 2002 study by the Modern Language Association, there was a 432% increase in ASL enrollment between 1998 and 2002. However, this growth in ASL use and the nature of hearing society has caused misconceptions and some confusion about ASL and ASL grammar rules.

The most common misconception about ASL is that it is a signed version of English. ASL is not English at all. ASL is a distinct language with its own syntax and grammar.

For new ASL students, the many grammar rules unique to ASL can become very confusing. Before we begin learning ASL grammar, it's very important that you understand the difference between ASL and other sign systems.

Make Sure You Are Learning ASL

When it comes to sign language, there are many different types. A lot of sign systems have been created for various reasons. For example, Signed English is primarily used for the education of deaf children.

Unlike ASL, sign systems are not real languages. So while you are learning ASL, it is important for you to be sure that you are truly learning American Sign Language and not an invented sign system. Below, you can read about the most common sign systems so that you are able to recognize them when you see them.

Signed English (SE)

Signed English, also known as SE, is a visual representation of English. Unlike ASL, the grammar in SE follows English word order and one word in English equals one sign in SE. There are many add-ons in this system as well, such as suffixes, prefixes, tenses, and endings. You may also see compound words expressed as separate signs. For example, instead of using the ASL sign for "butterfly," you may see someone use the signs for "butter" and "fly" used separately in sequential order. SE is used mostly in educational settings to teach English and build reading and writing skills.

Contact Signing/Pidgin Signed English (PSE)

Pidgin Signed English (also known as "contact signing") is a sign system that uses ASL signs in English word order. PSE is often used when Deaf and hearing people communicate in sign language. It can be described as a "middle ground" between English and ASL. PSE is not a real language—it just follows English word order while using ASL signs.

Cued Speech

Cued Speech was developed in 1966 by R. Orin Cornett at Gallaudet University in Washington D.C. The cues consist of eight handshapes used in four different positions. These cues are used in combination with the natural mouth movements that occur during speech. Cued Speech helps deaf individuals while lipreading to clarify similar sounds.

Total Communication (TC)

Total Communication uses sign, mime, writing, speech, fingerspelling, pictures, or any other method that enables communication. The method used depends on the person and the situation. Total Communication is used most often in education so deaf children are able to learn with whichever method works best for them.

Rochester Method

The Rochester Method is also known as Visible English and focuses on fingerspelling and speech. This method is based on English where each word in a sentence is fingerspelled.

This method isn't used much anymore because spelling out each word is very time consuming.

Moving Forward

As you move on in this book, you will learn certain signs and vocabulary as well as the grammar rules that make ASL a real language that is completely separate from English.

2 American Sign Language Signs and Vocabulary

In this section:

- **Fingerspelling**
- **Numbers**
- **Types of Signs**
- **Signs Without an English Translation**
- **Other Translations**
- **Idioms**
- **Sign Variation**

Learning ASL vocabulary is very important. It would be rather difficult to master ASL grammar without knowing some ASL vocabulary.

The best way to learn vocabulary is with a dictionary. Every ASL student should have access to several ASL dictionaries and study them on a regular basis to build up vocabulary.

This is my favorite printed dictionary:

American Sign Language Dictionary
by Martin L. Sternberg
This is the dictionary that I own and love. It's a huge book and explains more than 5,000 signs and has over 8,000 illustrations.

Here are my favorite online ASL dictionaries:

- Signing Savvy - This website claims to be the "most complete online sign language dictionary." Their dictionary has definitely become my favorite. It has high quality videos and a dictionary search feature. (**www.signingsavvy.com**)

- ASLPro - This is a video dictionary that has very big and clear videos that demonstrate a large amount of signs. (**www.aslpro.com**)

- ASL Browser - This is a site developed by the Communication Technology Laboratory at Michigan State University. It uses QuickTime videos to demonstrate a ton of ASL signs. However, some of the signs are outdated. (**commtechlab.msu.edu/sites/aslweb/browser.htm**)

- Lifeprint - This site has a rather large dictionary as well. It uses pictures instead of video which may be helpful if you have a slow internet connection. (**www.lifeprint.com**)

However, most ASL dictionaries do not fully explain some vocabulary *concepts* that are very important to know. These include how and when to sign certain groups of signs, the similarities between signs, some of the different types of signs, and more. In this section, I will explain some of the concepts that are not explained in most dictionaries.

Fingerspelling

Fingerspelling means spelling out words by using signs that correspond to the letters of the word. The signs that are used in ASL are from the American Manual Alphabet. This alphabet uses 22 handshapes in different positions or with certain movements to represent the 26 letters of the American alphabet.

Fingerspelling is only used about 10% of the time and is primarily used for:

- People's names
- Brand names
- Book and movie titles
- City and state names

American Sign Language Alphabet

Try not to use fingerspelling as your first choice when you don't know the sign. Instead, attempt to get your point across by combining other signs or using some other method.

However, there are many words that do not have corresponding signs in ASL. Go ahead and fingerspell if there is no other convenient way to explain what you are talking about.

Here are some tips for accurate fingerspelling:

- Keep your hand relaxed, to the right of your face (to the left if you are left handed), and below your chin.

- Make sure your palm is facing the person you are talking to.

- Keep your elbow down and close to your body.

- If you are right handed, you would fingerspell from left to right. If you are left handed, you would fingerspell from right to left.

- Try to break up the words into syllables. I have found that this makes fingerspelling a bit easier for most people. For example, instead of thinking of it as fingerspelling the whole word "vocabulary," think of it as fingerspelling "vo-cab-u-lar-y."

- Do not say or mouth the individual letters. I have found that most signers mouth the first and last syllable of the word and many mouth all of the syllables or the entire word.

- Aim for articulation, not speed. Right now, you just want to make sure you form the letters correctly so people will understand you.

- Try not to bounce your hand as you spell, or you will make someone very dizzy! Also allow a slight pause between words.

- For words with double letters, open your hand slightly between the letters. For open letters such as B and L, move your hand slightly to the right with a very slight bounce for the second letter. For words with a double Z (e.g. pizza), use the Bent-V-handshape to sign both Zs simultaneously.

- When reading fingerspelling, make sure you look at the whole word and not just the individual letters (just like in printed English). Look at the handshapes and movement. This will get you used to seeing words signed faster and faster. Some deaf people don't even fingerspell all the letters of a word.

Being able to sign and understand fingerspelling is very important when you are new to sign language and haven't learned a lot of signs. You will find that the more fluent you become in ASL, the less you will be relying on fingerspelling.

Lexicalized Fingerspelling

Lexicalized fingerspelling (sometimes called "loan signs") is fingerspelling that looks more like a sign rather than a fingerspelled word. These are 2-5 letter words that are commonly used and have their own special movements.

Here are some examples of words that are commonly lexicalized:

#AIR	#COOL	
#ALL	#DEPT	#JOB
#APT	#DID	#NG (no good)
#BACK	#DO	#TB (too bad)
#BANK	#DO-DO ("what do")	#REF
#BEACH	#DOG	#VEG
#BURN	#EARLY	#WHAT
#BUS	#FIX	#WHEN
#BUSY	#GAS	#WHY
#CAR	#HA	#WOW
#CLUB	#HURT	#YES

The main differences between a lexicalized sign and fingerspelled word are that lexicalized signs can have different handshapes, movements, palm orientations, and locations. For example, for the lexicalized sign #BACK, it would be signed quicker, toward a referent, and with only the "BCK" or "BAK" handshapes, where the "C" and "A" are normally not fully formed.

Another example would be #WHAT, where #WHAT is signed closer to your hip area in front of you with only the "WT" handshapes. The "W" is signed with your palm facing away from you, and your hand twists into the "T" with your palm facing toward you. And sometimes, it is signed with a slight "H" between the "W" and "T" handshapes.

You would normally use the lexicalized version of a sign if:

1. You want to emphasize a point.

2. You want to use directionality (e.g. "give-#BACK" (signing toward a specific referent).

3. You want to make a comparison (spell on different hands).

#BACK

Abbreviations

Many common words have been abbreviated with the manual alphabet. It is words like these that become lexicalized over time.

Here are some examples:

- AC (Air Conditioning)

- AVE (Avenue)

- BBQ (Barbeque)

- BLVD (Boulevard)

- CD (Compact Disc)

- DVD (Digital Video Disc)

- HS (High School)

- ID (Identification)

- OT (Overtime)

States

The states of the U.S. have their own abbreviations. When discussing them, you would use either the accepted sign for that state or these abbreviations:

AL	Alabama	MT	Montana
AK	Alaska	NE	Nebraska
AZ	Arizona	NV	Nevada
AR	Arkansas	NH	New Hampshire
CA	California	NJ	New Jersey
CO	Colorado	NM	New Mexico
CT	Connecticut	NY	New York
DE	Delaware	NC	North Carolina
FL	Florida	ND	North Dakota
GA	Georgia	OH	Ohio
HI	Hawaii	OK	Oklahoma
ID	Idaho	OR	Oregon
IL	Illinois	PA	Pennsylvania
IN	Indiana	RI	Rhode Island
IA	Iowa	SC	South Carolina
KS	Kansas	SD	South Dakota
KY	Kentucky	TN	Tennessee
LA	Louisiana	TX	Texas
ME	Maine	UT	Utah
MD	Maryland	VT	Vermont
MA	Massachusetts	VA	Virginia
MI	Michigan	WA	Washington
MN	Minnesota	WV	West Virginia
MS	Mississippi	WI	Wisconsin
MO	Missouri	WY	Wyoming

Calendar Months

The months of the year are also signed using fingerspelling. Each month has an abbreviation. Months with five letters or less are usually fully spelled out.

J-A-N	January	J-U-L-Y	July
F-E-B	February	A-U-G	August
M-A-R-C-H	March	S-E-P-T	September
A-P-R-I-L	April	O-C-T	October
M-A-Y	May	N-O-V	November
J-U-N-E	June	D-E-C	December

Numbers

Numbers are signed differently depending on what you are signing. In this section, I will explain the different types of numbers and how they are signed.

Cardinal Numbers

Cardinal numbers are pretty self explanatory. These are the numbers used for counting.

TWO

Numbers 1-5 can be signed with your palm either back (toward you) or forward (away from you).

SEVEN

Numbers 6-9 are signed with your palm forward and touching your fingertips to the tip of your thumb—last finger for 6, ring finger for 7, middle finger for 8, and index finger for 9.

TEN

Number 10 is signed by shaking a "thumbs up" handshape.

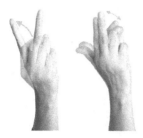

TWELVE/THIRTEEN

Numbers 11-15 are signed with your palm back. 11 is signed by flicking your index finger twice, 12 is signed by flicking your index and middle fingers twice, and 13-15 are signed by making the handshape of the number and moving your fingers toward you twice.

SEVENTEEN

Numbers 16-19 are signed either by starting with your palm back and twisting forward twice, or by combining the number with the sign for "10."

TWENTY

Number 20 is a standalone sign and is made with your index finger and thumb tapping together with all of your other fingers down.

THIRTY-FIVE

Numbers with 2-digits are generally signed by signing the first number and then the second number. For example, 35 would be signed as "3-5," with your palm facing forward. Numbers 21 and 23-29 are signed using the L-handshape for the "2" digit (e.g. "L-6" for 26).

FORTY

Numbers 30, 40, 50, 60, etc. are signed with your palm forward combining the number with the sign for "0."

THIRTY-THREE

Numbers 22, 33, 44, 55, etc. are signed with your palm forward and taking the number and bouncing it twice by bending your wrist.

ONE-HUNDRED

Number 100 is signed by using modified roman numerals. You would sign "1" then the letter "C."

THREE-HUNDRED

Numbers 200, 300, 400, 500, 600, 700, 800, and 900 can be signed using the method above or by taking the number and bending your fingers twice into a claw-like shape.

ONE-HUNDRED-TWO

Numbers between the hundreds can be signed in two different ways. For example, for 102, you can either sign "1-C-2" or "1-0-2." Both are acceptable.

TWO-THOUSAND

Numbers 1000, 2000, 3000, 4000 etc. are also signed by using modified roman numerals. You sign the number and then touch the letter "M" to your upward-facing palm. For example, for 1000, you would sign "1" and then touch the letter "M" to your palm. This is commonly slightly modified to be more of a "bent hand" handshape than an "M".

ONE-THOUSAND-TWENTY-THREE

Numbers between the thousands are signed with the "M" sign after the first number. For example, for the number 1023, you would sign "1-M-23."

TWO-MILLION

Numbers 1 million, 2 million, etc. are signed the same as the thousands, except instead of touching the "M" to your palm once, you would touch it to your palm twice, moving it closer to the tips of your fingers the second time.

TWO-BILLION

Numbers 1 billion, 2 billion, etc. are signed the same as the millions, except you touch the "M" to your palm three times (moving it forward twice).

Numbers over 1 trillion (and sometimes billion) are commonly fingerspelled or lexicalized (e.g. #BILL, #TRILL, #ZILL).

Ordinal Numbers

Numbers 1st-9th (numbers in a series) are signed by forming the handshape of the number and twisting your wrist with your palm twisting forward to inward.

Numbers 1st-9th (in a competitive tournament (e.g. a race)) are signed like the numbers in a series, except more horizontally.

Every number after 9th is signed by fingerspelling T-H after the number. Even though English gives a number such as 32 an "nd" ending to make 32nd, all numbers after 9th in ASL use "T-H" afterward.

Summary:

1st-9th = "(number) + (Wrist Twist)"

9th+ = "(number) + T-H"

2nd (series)   *10th*

Money

Money numbers are used for amounts of money (dollars and cents).

Amounts of money under one dollar (e.g. $0.75) are signed by combining the sign CENT with the number. You can sign these numbers two different ways: (1) Sign CENT with the handshape of the number (two digit numbers can be signed with the first digit as the beginning handshape and the second digit as the ending handshape), or (2) Sign CENT and then the number.

The signs for $1.00-$9.00 are signed by forming the number handshape with your hand, and twisting your hand from palm facing forward to palm facing inward (similar to ordinal numbers). These are also commonly seen signed more horizontally.

You sign amounts of money over $9.00 (e.g. $15.00) by signing the number then the sign DOLLAR.

To sign dollars and cents (e.g. $2.75), you would first sign the dollar amount and then the cent amount. For example, you could sign "2 + (Wrist Twist)" and then "75" with your palm facing forward to show 2 dollars and 75 cents. For the cents, you could also sign "CENT(with 75 handshape)" or "CENT 75". The most popular way to sign this would be "2(Wrist Twist) + 75". The CENT sign is normally dropped when signing money in context.

Another example would be $17.85. You would first sign "17" or "17 DOLLAR" and then "85", "CENT(with 85 handshape)" or "CENT 85". The most popular way to sign this would be "17 + 85". The DOLLAR sign is normally dropped when signing money in context.

Keep in mind that money numbers are always signed with your palm facing forward (with the exception of the inward wrist twist).

Summary:

$0.01-0.99 = "CENT(with number handshape)" or "CENT + (number)"

$1.00-$9.00 = "(number) + (Wrist Twist)"

$9.00+ = "(number) + DOLLAR"

$2.75 = "2(Wrist Twist) + 75" or "2(Wrist Twist) + CENT(with 75 handshape)" or "2(Wrist Twist) + CENT 75"

$15.25 = "15 + 25" or "15 DOLLAR + 25" or "15 DOLLAR + CENT(with 25 handshape)" or "15 DOLLAR + CENT 25"

35 cents

2 dollars

13 dollars

$13.35

Age

Age numbers are used when talking about a person's age. Age numbers are formed by combining the sign OLD with the number. Ages 1-9 are signed by signing OLD with the handshape of the number with your palm facing forward.

For ages 10-19, you sign OLD first, then the number. The sign for OLD is typically shortened to be the 1-handshape touching your chin.

For ages 20 and up, you sign OLD with the first number as the starting handshape (near your chin) and the second number as the ending handshape (in front of your chest).

| *3 years old* | *11 years old* | *35 years old* |

When talking about the members of a family, you will usually rank them by age with your non-dominant hand. This is normally used for discussing siblings and children.

Your highest finger represents the oldest person while your lowest represents the youngest (normally your thumb and pinkie finger). You can also use these fingers as references to point to as you continue talking about the family members.

Example of Ranking

60's-90's Wrist Tilt

Certain numbers between 67 and 98 are unique because your wrist tilts a certain way to sign them.

For the numbers 67, 78, 79, and 89, your hand will tilt toward you. For the numbers 76, 86, 87, 96, 97, and 98, your hand will tilt away from you.

87

Time

The signs for 1-12 o'clock are signed by first signing TIME then the number. For 1-9 o'clock you shake the number a little bit (this is commonly shortened to have the number start when you touch your wrist for TIME instead of signing TIME and the number separate).

For times such as 9:08, you first sign TIME and the number for the hour (numbers 1-9 with palm facing out, and numbers 10-12 with one movement). Then, slightly to the right, you sign the numbers for the minutes. The minutes are signed how they are said in English. For example, for 9:15, you would sign, "TIME 9" and then slightly to the right, "15". If it is only 1-9 minutes after the hour, sign ZERO before the minutes.

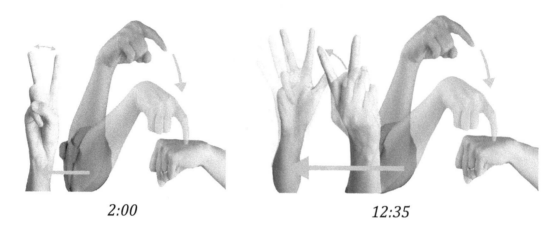

| 2:00 | 12:35 |

Fractions

Fractions are signed exactly as they look. First sign the top number (the numerator), move your hand downward slightly, and sign the bottom number (the denominator). For example, to sign ½, you would sign "1," move your hand downward slightly, and sign "2." For numbers 6-9, your palm will face inward.

One Half (1/2)

Height

Height is signed exactly the opposite of fractions. The number of feet is signed first, you move your hand upward slightly, and then sign the number of inches.

5'3"

Measurements

Measurements are usually signed by first signing the number and then fingerspelling the measurement or English measurement abbreviation.

Length

1 foot = "1" + "F-T"
1 inch = "1" + "I-N-C-H"
1 meter = "1" + "M"
1 yard = "1" + "Y-A-R-D"
1 millimeter = "1" + "M-M"
1 centimeter = "1" + "C-M"
1 kilometer = "1" + "K-M"

Volume

1 teaspoon = "1" + "T-S-P"
1 tablespoon = "1" + "T-B"
1 cup = "1" + "C-U-P"
1 ounce = "1" + "O-Z"
1 pint = "1" + "P-T"

1 quart = "1" + "Q-T"
1 gallon = "1" + "G-A-L"
1 milliliter = "1" + "M-L"
1 liter = "1" + "L-I-T-E-R"

Weight

1 gram = "1" + "G-R-A-M"
1 pound = "1" + "L-B"

Other Numbers

When you are signing a year, you would sign it as you would say it in English. For 1987, you would sign 19 and then 87. For the years 2000 and on, signers are signing them as 2-000 (sliding your hand with the 0 handshape to indicate multiple digits) or 2-00-1 (sliding your hand for the 0's).

Some signers use the sign for THOUSAND as part of the sign for years 2000 and up. And some sign them as two-digit numbers (e.g. 2001 signed as "TWENTY ZERO ONE").

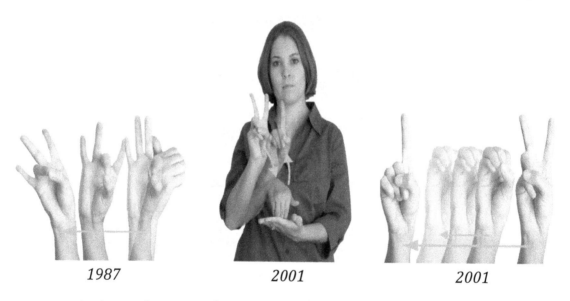

| 1987 | 2001 | 2001 |

When you are signing a phone number or address, you keep your palm facing away from you and sign each number. For example, the phone number 102-7442 is shown below. When signing a phone number, insert a short pause where the hyphen would be.

102-7442

You can also combine two-digit numbers. For example, you can sign the address 1219 as "TWELVE NINETEEN".

Letters and Numbers

When you are having a conversation involving both letters and numbers, you would slightly shake the numbers back and forth and sign the letters normally. This way, you are able to distinguish between the two.

Types of Signs

In ASL, there are groups of signs that share similar characteristics. Knowing these similarities can help you understand sign variations and new vocabulary in context.

Gender Signs

Gender signs tend to be signed in certain locations, which makes them easy to specify. Most male signs are formed on or near the forehead while most female signs are formed on or near the cheek or chin.

Signs for FATHER and MOTHER

For example, FATHER is signed by touching the tip of your thumb to your head, while MOTHER is signed by touching the tip of your thumb to your chin.

This is important to keep in mind because pronouns in ASL are gender-neutral. For example, you sign both "he" and "she" by pointing your index finger off to the side. They are signed exactly the same. Gender is normally established with a clear male or female sign (like MOTHER or FATHER) to clarify the meaning before using a pronoun sign.

Iconic Signs

When signs look like the word they are representing, these are called *iconic* signs. These signs can often be recognized by people who don't know basic sign language. The sign for ELEPHANT is signed like an elephant's trunk. The sign for SWIMMING looks like a small swimming motion. There are many signs like this.

Some signs seem to be arbitrary when you first see them, but when you look at the root, they become more iconic. For example, the sign for HOME is made by placing your hand on your lips, then on your head. This represents where someone eats and sleeps.

Compound Signs

Compound signs are two signs that when put together create a different meaning than either sign alone. You need to use both signs in order to create the meaning of the compound sign.

An English example of a compound word would be, "blackboard." This word combines the words "black" and "board" to create a word that doesn't have a meaning related to either of those words alone.

Here are some common ASL compound signs:

- EAT+MORNING = BREAKFAST
- EAT+AFTERNOON = LUNCH
- EAT+NIGHT = DINNER
- KNOW+CONTINUE = REMEMBER
- LEARN+AGENT = STUDENT
- THINK+OPPOSITE = DISAGREE
- BOY+BABY = SON
- GIRL+BABY = DAUGHTER
- BOY+SAME = BROTHER
- GIRL+SAME = SISTER

- BROTHER+SISTER = SIBLING
- MOTHER+FATHER = PARENTS
- JESUS+BOOK = BIBLE
- HOME+WORK = HOMEWORK

Many of these signs have developed over time and now look like one sign instead of two separate ones. For example, the sign BROTHER is made by signing BOY+SAME where BOY now has only one movement and SAME has a different palm orientation that looks more like the sign CORRECT.

This also happens in English when a compound word sounds like one word instead of two separate words. An example of this would be "cupboard" where "board" is pronounced differently than when said alone.

This change in production is called "assimilation" where the two signs fuse together over time.

The "Agent" Affix (the "Person Affix")

The agent affix is added to some signs to create compound signs that mean a person does something or is something.

For example, you would sign "TEACH AGENT" for the sign TEACHER. You could also sign "AMERICA AGENT" for the sign AMERICAN.

To make the AGENT affix, point both of your flat hands forward in front of your chest with your palms facing each other. Then, move both of your hands down at the same time.

"AGENT"

TEACHER

Keep in mind that you cannot add the AGENT affix to all "person" signs. This only works for a certain number of them.

Loan Signs

Loan signs are signs that are borrowed from other sign languages.

Many loan signs that are borrowed from other countries are the signs that the deaf people in that country use to refer to their country.

For example, the American Sign Language sign for CHINA used to be twisting your index finger next to your eye—it referred to the eye shape of Chinese people. That sign is now seen as inappropriate, so ASL has borrowed the sign for CHINA from Chinese Sign Language. We now use the same sign that they use for the word CHINA. It is signed by pointing to your left chest area, then right chest area, then right hip area.

Name Signs

Name signs are used to identify and refer to people. This eliminates the need to fingerspell a person's name repeatedly. Usually a Deaf child receives a name sign when they start attending a residential school. Children with Deaf parents receive a name sign at birth.

There are three types of name signs used by Deaf people—arbitrary, descriptive, and a hybrid of both. Arbitrary name signs use the first letter of the person's name (e.g. tapping the L-handshape on your shoulder). Descriptive name signs are based on one of the person's physical characteristics (e.g. indicating a mole on your face). And hybrid name signs are a combination of the two (e.g. tapping the L-handshape on your face to indicate a mole).

Hearing sign language students normally receive a hybrid name sign in an in-person sign language class to use in the classroom. However, you're not supposed to use these name signs outside of the classroom.

You can only receive a real name sign from a Deaf person once you have been involved in the Deaf community. You cannot create your own name sign—it must be given to you by a Deaf person. And even if you do receive a name sign, you should always introduce yourself by fingerspelling your full name.

Signs for "No"

The word "no" in ASL is very different from English. There are different signs for the word "no," while there is only one word for "no" in English.

To answer "no" to a yes or no question, use the sign NO. For example, you would use the sign NO for sentences like "No, I don't like pickles" and "No, I like pickles."

NO

To form a negative statement, use the sign NOT. The sign NOT would be used to form a statement such as, "I am not driving."

NOT

To sign a statement like "I have no children," or "There are no more chairs available," you would use the sign for NONE.

NONE

With any negative statement, you need to keep shaking your head throughout the statement. You will learn more about negative non-manual markers in a later section.

Initialized Signs

An initialized sign is one that uses the handshape of the first letter of the word. Many initialized signs are only used in sign systems, so overusing initialization is generally frowned upon in the Deaf Community.

However, many initialized signs are fully accepted as part of ASL. Here is a list of several initialized signs that are accepted as being ASL signs:

ALGEBRA	ELEVATOR	OFFICE	SATURDAY
ATTITUDE	FAMILY	OPINION	SOCIETY
BOSS	FRIDAY	ORGANIZATION	STATE
BEER	FRUIT	PATIENT	TEAM
BIOLOGY	GEOMETRY	POLICY	THURSDAY
BLUE	GREEN	PRINCIPLE	TRIGONOMETRY
CAFETERIA	GROUP	PRINCE	TUESDAY
CALCULUS	HOSPITAL	PRINCESS	VEGETABLE
CHARACTER	KING	PURPLE	WATER
CHEMISTRY	LAW	QUEEN	WEDNESDAY
CHRISTIAN	LORD	RESTAURANT	WINE
CLASS	MATH	RESTROOM	YELLOW
COACH	MONDAY	ROOM	
COUSIN	NURSE	ROSE	

GROUP

If there is both an initialized and non-initialized sign for a certain word, use the non-initialized sign (e.g. SINGLE). This will be more accepted in the Deaf Community.

Signs without an English Translation

In ASL, there are many signs that do not have an exact English translation. These are signs that need a short explanation so you will know how and when to use them.

They are considered to be "more ASL" than if you were to use other vocabulary to sign the same thing. Many signers mistakenly use English equivalents of these signs, which almost always mean something completely different in ASL.

Below, I have outlined some of the most common of these signs that you should know for everyday conversation. This way, you can make sure that you use the correct ASL sign for these sentences.

FINISH-TOUCH

The signs FINISH and TOUCH are used to mean you have already visited a certain place. This is like saying "been to" in English.

For example, you may ask someone, "FINISH-TOUCH NEW-YORK YOU?" to mean "Have you ever been to New York?"

FINISH-TOUCH

TEND-TO

The sign TEND-TO can be used to explain that you usually do something. For example, you may sign, "MORNING ME TEND-TO BRUSH-TEETH."

TEND-TO is also more commonly used to mean "prone to" in sentences like, "He is prone to mischief."

TEND-TO

NAME-SHINE

You may see the sign NAME-SHINE used to describe someone as having a very good reputation. This sign is considered to be "*very* ASL," so I thought I would share it with you.

For example, someone may ask if you know Thomas Hopkins Gallaudet and you could reply, "GALLAUDET(name sign), NAME-SHINE" with the topical and affirmative facial expressions.

NAME-SHINE

Do you mind...?

To ask someone if they mind, you would use the sign don't-MIND.

For example, you could ask "don't-MIND ME INTERRUPT?" with the yes/no facial expression to ask "Would it be ok if I interrupt?"

don't-MIND?

FINISH

You can use the sign for FINISH in many different ways.

For example, if you are explaining what you do in the morning, you could sign "MORNING ME GET-UP, EAT BREAKFAST FINISH, BRUSH-TEETH FINISH, DRIVE SCHOOL."

You can sign "HOMEWORK FINISH YOU?" to ask if the person has finished their homework.

You can sign "SURGERY FINISH, SHE BETTER NOW" to mean that the woman is better now that she has had surgery.

You can also sign something like "ME NOT-YET FINISH WASH CAR" to mean "I haven't finished washing the car."

FINISH

Other Translations

Here are some more English words (and prefixes) that don't directly translate into ASL:

English	ASL
This is for real/no joke	TRUE BUSINESS
Alphabet	ABC
Grammar School	ELEMENTARY SCHOOL
Public School	MAINSTREAM or HEARING SCHOOL
Admire, love	KISS-FIST
Because	WHY? (rhetorical question)
Sibling	BROTHER/SISTER
Parents	MOM/DAD
Knock it off	FINISH ("FSH" mouth movement)
What for?	FOR-FOR?
un-/dis-	NOT
("disbelieve")	("NOT BELIEVE")
mis-	WRONG
("misjudge")	("WRONG JUDGE")
re-	AGAIN
("reuse")	("AGAIN USE")

Idioms

An example of an idiom in English is the phrase "kick the bucket," which means "to die." ASL, however, does not use English idioms. If you were to sign "RAIN CAT DOG" this would actually *mean* cats and dogs are falling from the sky in ASL. So, if you want to sign an English idiom, you need to sign what the idiom actually *means* instead of the exact words.

ASL does have its own idioms, though. One idiom would be "TRAIN GONE(CL:G(train)"fade out of sight")" which directly translates into "train go sorry" in English. "Train go sorry," of course, doesn't mean anything in English, but in ASL the sign means, "Sorry, you missed it. I am not going to repeat what I said."

Sign Variation

It is important to note that variation is very common in ASL. Signs can vary for many different reasons: the region, the situation, the age of the signer, the change in technology, etc.

Most of the time, if you see a word signed differently, both versions are correct, they are just variations. I teach from the variations I have come to learn and use. Being involved in the Deaf community and having a lot of vocabulary dictionaries and resources at your fingertips can help you learn the many variations of signs, and choose which variations you want to use.

Moving Forward

ASL Vocabulary is a very important part of ASL grammar. I have shown you the important vocabulary concepts that aren't always mentioned and it's now up to you to consult an ASL dictionary and increase your vocabulary further! After you have learned some ASL vocabulary, it will be a lot easier to learn and understand the ASL grammar rules.

3 American Sign Language
Grammar

To put it simply, grammar is a set of rules for using a language. The grammar of a language includes the phonology, morphology, and syntax of that language.

A language's grammar is determined by the group of people who use that language. The main users of American Sign Language are the members of the Deaf community. The way that the Deaf community uses ASL is what constitutes ASL grammar.

American Sign Language has its own grammar system. This means that ASL has its own rules for phonology, morphology, and syntax.

In the rest of this book, I will explain all of the important rules you need to know about ASL grammar.

You will learn:

- **The rules of ASL phonology and how signs are formed.**

- **The rules of ASL morphology and how signs are inflected to create meaning.**

- **The rules of ASL syntax and how to form correct sentences in ASL.**

This book contains what you need to know in order to accurately sign in American Sign Language.

4 American Sign Language
Phonology

In this section:

- **The Five Sign Parameters**
- **Parameter #1: Handshape**
- **Parameter #2: Movement**
- **Parameter #3: Palm Orientation**
- **Parameter #4: Location**
- **Parameter #5: Non-Manual Markers**

In language, phonology is the study of the smallest part of the language that conveys meaning. In spoken languages, like English, a phoneme is a unit of sound that conveys meaning.

For example, if you change the "a" in "sad" to "o," you would create "sod," which has a completely different meaning.

In ASL, the smallest parts of the language, the phonemes, are handshape, movement, palm orientation, location, and facial expression. If you change any of these parameters of a sign, then you have changed the meaning of the sign.

For example, if you change the movement of the sign CHAIR to only one movement instead of two, you have just created the sign SIT.

The Five Sign Parameters

Just like how we see English words as the arrangement of letters, there are five basic sign language elements that make up each sign. If any of these parameters are changed when creating a sign, the meaning of the sign can change.

The first four elements are:

- **Handshape** – This is the shape of your hand that is used to create the sign.

- **Movement** – This is the movement of the handshape that makes the sign.

- **Palm orientation** – This is the orientation of your palm when making the sign.

- **Location** – This is the location of the sign on or in front of your body.

There is also a fifth element that has recently been included with this list:

- **Non-manual Markers** – This is the various facial expressions or body movements that are used to create meaning.

American Sign Language is a very expressive language, and understanding these elements will give you a better understanding of how signs are made and what makes them different.

Parameter #1: Handshape

All signs are formed using a specific handshape. If you change the handshape of a sign, you can change the meaning of the sign. For example, if you change the handshape of the sign SCIENCE to a B-handshape, you would be signing the initialized sign BIOLOGY. So, it is important to know how to accurately form the handshape(s) of each sign.

Below are some of the common handshapes used in American Sign Language:

V Handshape   *Inverted V*   *Bent V*   *Closed Hand*

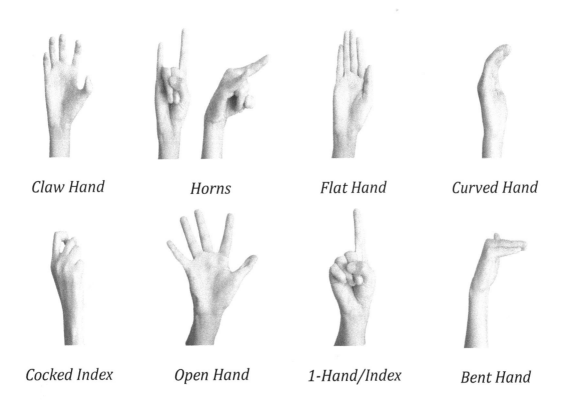

Claw Hand   Horns   Flat Hand   Curved Hand

Cocked Index   Open Hand   1-Hand/Index   Bent Hand

ABCOS15

The handshapes "ABCOS15" are the handshapes that are formed by your non-dominant hand while signing. You will notice that for two-handed signs where only one hand moves (a non-symmetrical sign), your non-dominant will most likely be using one of these handshapes. These are handshapes your non-dominant hand uses as a stationary base for your moving dominant hand.

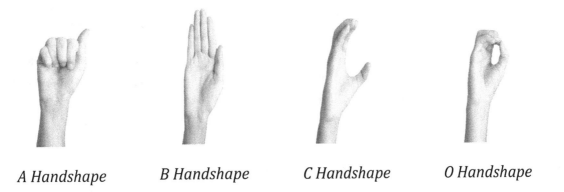

A Handshape   B Handshape   C Handshape   O Handshape

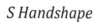

S Handshape	*1 Handshape*	*5 Handshape*

Parameter #2: Movement

The movement of a sign is the action that is used to create the sign. The movement can be in a circle, up and down, forward or backward, etc. If you change the movement of a sign, you can change the meaning of a sign.

For example, for the sign CHAIR, you move your dominant hand down twice and for the sign SIT, you move your dominant hand down once. A simple change of movement changes the meaning of that sign.

You will also notice that movements of some sequential signs have fused together over time. For example, the phrase "GOOD MORNING" is signed using one movement instead of two separate movements for each sign—your dominant hand doesn't stop moving until after MORNING.

Your Dominant Hand

You have a dominant and non-dominant hand. If you are right-handed, your right hand is your dominant hand. If you are left-handed, your left hand is your dominant hand.

If you are ambidextrous, choose one hand to use as your dominant hand, and stick with it. However, if possible, I would recommend choosing your right hand as your dominant hand because most ASL dictionaries are illustrated this way.

There are three types of signs when it comes to what hand you will use:

1. **One-handed signs:** Use only your dominant hand.

2. **Two-handed signs where both hands move:** Move both your dominant and non-dominant hand. These signs normally use the same handshape and movement for both hands.

3. **Two-handed signs where one hand moves:** Move your dominant hand and keep your non-dominant hand stationary.

One-handed sign   *Two-handed sign with both hands moving*   *Two-handed sign with one hand moving*

More often than not, your non-dominant hand will never move unless your dominant hand is moving the same way. This is very important when you move into more complex signing. You don't want to get confused!

Parameter #3: Palm Orientation

The palm orientation of a sign refers to the position of the palms of your hands and the direction they are facing. If you change the palm orientation of a sign, you can change the meaning of the sign.

For example, the sign MY is made by placing your palm on your chest and the sign YOUR is made by facing your palm toward the other person. A simple change in palm orientation changes the meaning of that sign.

It is also important to know how to refer to the palm orientation of a sign:

 **Forward** – Palm is facing away from your body

Inward – Palm is facing toward your body

Horizontal – Palm is parallel to the floor

Palm toward palm – Palms are facing each other

Palm to palm – Palms are applied to each other

Parameter #4: Location

The location of a sign is where you place and form the sign in your signing area. If you change the location of a sign, you can change the meaning of a sign.

Some examples of locations include:

- In front of your body,
- Your head,
- Your face (forehead, eyes, temples, ear, nose, cheek, mouth, or chin),
- Your neck,
- Your shoulder, chest, or stomach,
- Your arm or elbow,
- Your waist,
- Your wrist, and
- Your non-dominant hand. In this case, your non-dominant hand will most likely use one of the ABCOS15 handshapes.

For example, the sign MOTHER is formed by tapping the thumb of your open-five hand on your chin, and the sign FATHER is formed by tapping the thumb of your open-five hand on your forehead. This simple change in location changes the meaning of the sign.

Signing Area

Your signing area is in the shape of a pyramid starting from the top of your head, down past your shoulders, and ending in a horizontal line at your waist. Unless you are signing a formal speech for a large audience, your signs shouldn't move outside of this area.

The space in the center of the chest is called the sightline. The sightline is where you would focus your eyes on a signer. This enables you to use your peripheral vision to see the signer's hands and facial expressions at the same time. Make sure to try to wear solid colored clothing (without designs) when signing—it is easier on the eyes.

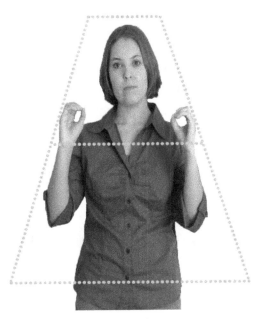

Signing Area

Parameter #5: Non-Manual Markers (NMM)

Non-Manual Markers are very important in American Sign Language. They consist of the various facial expressions and body movements that are added to signs to create meaning. Non-manual markers can be facial expressions, head shakes, head nods, head tilts, shoulder shrugs, etc.

And not only do non-manual markers have a very important role in ASL grammar, but if you do not use any non-manual markers or facial expressions, your audience may not understand what you are signing, or worse, they may get bored very quickly. In English, this would be like speaking in a monotone voice.

Facial Expressions

Facial expressions are the non-manual markers that refer only to the expressions on your face. The meaning of your sign can be affected by the type of facial expression you use while signing it.

For example, if you use an exaggerated facial expression while signing the word HAPPY, then you are signing "*very* happy." This also works to change FUNNY into "*very* funny." In ASL, you will notice that less signs are used with more facial expression to get the same message across in a more clear and visual way. For example, you really would never sign, "VERY HAPPY." The VERY can come across in your facial expression so you would only have to sign HAPPY.

Facial expressions can also determine what type of question you are asking. If you raise your eyebrows while asking a question, you are asking a yes or no question. If you lower your eyebrows while asking a question, you are asking a question that requires more than a yes or no answer (generally a "wh" word question).

Yes/No Question

"Wh" Word Question

Facial expressions also add clarity to what you mean when you are signing. Some signs even require a certain facial expression in order to sign them. For example, the only difference between the signs LATE and NOT-YET is the facial expression. NOT-YET is signed with your tongue hanging out slightly over your bottom teeth. Without this facial expression, the meaning of the sign changes.

And there are over 100 mouth movements in ASL that are used to convey an adverb, adjective, or another more descriptive meaning when signing certain ASL words. Here are some examples:

"cha"   *"pah"*

"fsh"

English	ASL
I drank a large cup of soda.	__"cha" ME FINISH DRINK LARGE SODA
I finally finished my term paper!	_____t ___"pah" TERM PAPER, ME FINALLY FINISH
I finished washing the car.	__"fsh" ME FINISH WASH-CAR
The chocolate melted all over the place.	_"thh" CHOCOLATE MELT
I broke the phone.	__"bro" ME BROKE PHONE
I finished very recently.	_____"cs" ME RECENT FINISH
She doesn't pay attention when she drives.	__"th" SHE DRIVE
Yesterday, I was just walking along like normal.	_"mm" YESTERDAY ME WALK
I saw a huge crowd of people.	"cheeks _____puffed" ME SEE PEOPLE HORDES-OF
She is very thin.	"lips _pursed" SHE THIN
She struggled a lot with math.	_____t _"sta-sta-sta" MATH, SHE STRUGGLE++

Body Language/Role Shifting

Body language is also one of the many non-manual markers. You would use body language for things like role shifting.

Role shifting is very much fun in ASL. It's like acting. Role shifting is when you take on the "role" of another person and show what that person said, did, or felt. Essentially, you can sign a whole story using role shifting.

Instead of signing "SHE SAID" and then "HE SAID," you can turn your body slightly to the left to sign the comments of one person and then turn your body slightly to the right to sign the comments of the other person. When discussing a ball game, you can be the person throwing the ball and then become the other person catching the ball. You can even show a whole conversation between multiple people simply by using body shift and eye gaze. Essentially, you can "role play" each person.

You need to be sure to include the appropriate facial expressions and other non-manual markers when role playing each person. For example, if you are showing a conversation between a parent and a child, you would take on the characteristics of the parent and gaze downward when you shift one way, and take on the characteristics of the child and gaze upward when you shift the other way.

This is also essential if you are showing people in different positions or locations. You would need to be able to show if someone is standing or sitting, laying down or kneeling, etc. For example, because you can't turn and sign, you can show that you are talking to someone sitting behind you in a car by using eye gaze and pointing to their location before taking on their characteristics.

Role shifting is difficult to explain in a book. The best way to practice and understand role shifting is to watch how signers tell stories and see it in action.

Moving Forward

ASL phonology is the most basic part of ASL grammar. You have learned the parts that make up each individual sign. Next, you will be learning how to add inflection and change those signs into nouns, verbs, adverbs, etc.

5 American Sign Language
Morphology

In this section:
- **Inflection (Adverbs)**
- **Noun-Verb Pairs**
- **Classifiers**
- **Verbs**
- **Time**

In language, morphology is the study of the forms and formations of words. A morpheme is the smallest indivisible unit of syntax that retains meaning.

For example, in English, the word "threateningly" consists of four morphemes: "threat," which is a noun; "en," which changes the noun into a verb; "ing," which changes it into an adjective; and "ly" which changes it into an adverb.

In ASL, there are no signs for affixes like "en," "ing," "ly," etc. to change the meaning of words. Instead, ASL uses non-manual markers, changes in parameters, and other signs to indicate tense, degree, intensity, plurality, aspect, and more.

Inflection (Adverbs)

Adverbs can modify an adjective, a verb, or another adverb to indicate time, place, manner, cause, or intensity. For example, English words like "quickly," "boldly," and "slowly" are adverbs.

In ASL, there are no separate signs for adverbs. Adverbs are created by adding inflection to a sign. Inflection can include varying the intensity or speed of signing or by incorporating facial expression.

For example, the sign for WALK can be made quickly or slowly to indicate how the person is walking, LIGHT-BLUE is made by signing BLUE with a slight wrist turning motion, and SMART becomes BRILLIANT and PRETTY becomes BEAUTIFUL when signs are exaggerated.

Instead of signing "ME VERY HAPPY," you would sign "ME ***HAPPY***," signing HAPPY in an exaggerated fashion with a larger movement and increased facial expression.

Here are some ways you can inflect a sign:

1. Use a more intense facial expression
2. Sign faster, slower, or sharper
3. Sign using a larger movement
4. Nod your head faster, slower, or sharper
5. Shake your head faster, slower, or sharper

This is also where the many natural ASL mouth movements can be used. For example, instead of just signing, "ME WANT LARGE SODA," you can sign "ME WANT LARGE("CHA") SODA" with the "CHA" mouth movement to mean a "gigantic" or "huge" soda.

Different signs are normally inflected in different ways. The inflection that you choose to use will depend mostly on the sign you are using.

Noun-Verb Pairs

Noun-verb pairs are signs that use the same handshape, location, and orientation, but use a different movement to indicate the difference between the noun and verb.

In English, the difference between a noun and a verb can be expressed with an affix like "threat" versus "threaten." In ASL, the difference is expressed by movement.

A signed verb usually has a single, continuous movement while a noun usually has a double movement.

An example of a noun/verb pair is the sign for CHAIR and the sign for SIT. To sign CHAIR, you would do the motion twice. To sign SIT, you would do the motion once. Another example of a noun/verb pair is the sign for AIRPLANE and the sign for FLY.

This even works for some words that are used in both forms. For example, in the sentence, "I need your help," "help" is a noun and has a double movement. In the sentence, "Help your mom," "help" is a verb and has a single movement.

CHAIR   SIT

Classifiers

Spoken languages like English are linear—they are expressed one word after the other. ASL, however, is a spatial language and is expressed in the space around you. Classifiers create depth as well as add clarity, movement, and details to conversations and explanations.

In ASL, it makes much more sense to create imaginary people, animals, or objects in your signing space and show what happens to them instead of explain every word in a linear fashion like you would in English.

The handshapes and movements of classifiers can represent people, animals, objects, etc. and show movements, shapes, actions, and locations. They can show a person walking, an animal chewing, someone driving, a car driving through the mountains—virtually anything!

In a sentence, a classifier is very similar to a pronoun. You cannot use a classifier in a sentence until you explain what the classifier represents. They are not standalone words. You need to establish the noun before you can apply the classifier.

An example of a classifier would be showing a person walking. You first have to establish this person as a referent in context and point to the referent, and then you can take the index finger of your dominant hand (the CL:1 classifier) and move it around your signing space. Whatever you do with this classifier is whatever the person is doing. You can also inflect the sign for added meaning. The faster or slower you move this classifier shows how fast or slow the person is doing an action. You can also use non-manual markers to show how the person is feeling while doing it. And because most classifier handshapes represent a whole person or object, you can combine classifiers like CL:1(person) with another classifier like CL:3(car) to show a person and a car and their locations relative to each other. Here are two examples of using classifiers with both hands at the same time:

TODAY TWO CAR (dh)CL:3(car)/(nh)CL:3(car)"drive toward each other and crash"

TODAY ME WALK CL:1(me)"walk forward" WRONG HAPPEN (2h)CL:F(thin pole) P-O-L-E (nh)CL:1(pole on ground)/ME (dh)CL:V-inv(me)"trip and fall"

There are an infinite number of classifiers that you can use. You can combine almost any handshape with any movement and location to create a classifier.

Classifiers are written like this: **CL:1 (person) "walking slow"**. The CL indicates that a classifier is being used, the 1 indicates the handshape, the parenthesis indicate what the classifier is representing, and the quotes indicate the inflection being used.

Here are some examples of handshapes and how they can be used for different types of classifiers:

CL:3 represents vehicles (e.g. cars, trains, boats, motorcycles, bicycles, etc.)

CL:1 represents long thin things (e.g. people, poles, sticks, etc.)

CL:C represents thick cylindrical items (e.g. glass, cup, cookies, etc.)

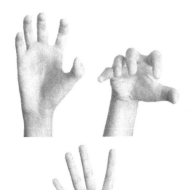

CL:5 in a claw-like form can represent a lot of something (e.g. crowd of people, pile of laundry, etc.) or things like a snowball or bush or (with palm down) a location of a city, in a flat-form can represent something flat without straight edges (e.g. a leaf), or in another form can represent something like a candle flame.

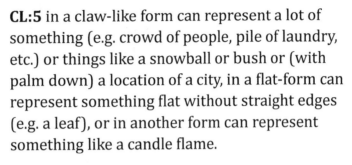

CL:V can represent people (e.g. two people walking, people sitting in a circle, etc.), bent at the knuckles can represent chairs or an animal moving (e.g. a circle of chairs, a dog sitting, etc.), or inverted can represent a person's legs (e.g. person walking, jumping, falling, dancing, etc.)

CL:L with two hands can represent small rectangular things (e.g. a check, a credit card, etc.), with two hands and the "L" bent at the knuckles can represent circular things (e.g. a small dish, a dinner plate, etc.)

CL:B represents flat things (a wall, roof, window, etc.), with palm down (bed, table, etc.), and with palm up (book, pan, magazine, etc.)

CL:4 can represent things like a long line of people, curtains, people moving in line, running water, etc.

CL:A with your thumb up represents an object in a certain location (e.g. a house, a lamp, etc.)

Here are some of the different types of classifiers that you can use:

- **Whole Classifiers:** These are classifiers where the handshape represents a whole object. For example, CL:3(car), CL:1(person), etc.

- **Surface Classifiers:** These are classifiers where the handshape is used to show the surface of something. For example, CL:B(wall), (2h)CL:B(hills), etc.

- **Instrument Classifiers:** These are classifiers where the handshapes show that you are holding something. For example, CL:C(holding cup), CL:S(hold hammer), CL:S(driving), etc.

- **Size Classifiers:** These are classifiers where the handshape shows the depth or width of something. For example, (2h)CL:C(thick vertical pole), (2h)CL:F(thin vertical pole), (2h)CL:L-curve(small plate), etc.

- **Amount Classifiers:** These are classifiers where the handshapes show the increase or decrease in the amount or volume of something. For example, CL:B-bent(liquid level decreasing), etc.

- **Shape Classifiers:** These are classifiers where the handshapes trace the exterior shape of something. For example, (2h)CL:B(large box shape), (2h)CL:L-curve(credit card), etc.

- **Location Classifiers:** These are classifiers where the location of the handshape represents the location of something. For example, CL:5-claw(city here), CL:A(house here), CL:5-claw(bush here), etc.

- **Gesture Classifiers:** These are classifiers where you use your body to act out something. For example, "stomp foot", "give hug", etc.

- **Body Classifiers:** These are classifiers where the handshape shows a part of your body doing an action. For example, CL:V(look around), (2h)CL:G(big smile), (2h) CL:B(foot stumble), etc.

- **Verb Classifiers:** These are classifiers that are used to show how something is doing an action. For example, CL:3(car)"drive down hill", CL:3(bicycle)"drive by", etc.

- **Plural Classifiers:** These are classifiers where the handshape and movement show that there is more than one of something. Some handshapes already indicate plurality, like CL:V(two people)"walking".

  However, you can indicate plurality with non-plural classifiers by using both hands in alternating, straight line/repeating, or opposite motions. Alternating motions indicate that the classifiers are not arranged in an orderly fashion. For example, (2h) CL:3(cars)"here, here, here, etc."

  Straight line/repeating motions (moving dominant hand and keeping non-dominant hand stationary as a referent) and opposite motions (starting together, then moving away from each other simultaneously) indicate they are arranged in an orderly fashion. For example, (2h)CL:4(people in line), (2h)CL:1(pencil)"(dh)lined up one right after the other", (2h)CL:5-claw(hordes-of people), (2h)CL:2(people sitting in a circle), etc.

An example of the vast use of classifiers could simply be discussing people throwing a ball back and forth. Balls can be different sizes, like a football, baseball, ping pong ball, tennis ball, etc., so your classifier chosen should reflect that. If it is a ball you can hold in your hand, you can use the CL:5-claw handshape to show someone holding it or use the same handshape during a "throw" gesture classifier to show someone throwing it.

CL:5-claw(ball)"throw ball"

You could also use role shifting to show who is throwing the ball to whom and the position of each person. For example, someone standing could be throwing the ball to someone sitting.

ME CL:1(me)"stand here" MY BROTHER (dh)CL:1(me)/(nh)CL:V-curve(brother)"sit across from me" ME CL:5-claw(ball)"throw ball" MY BROTHER ("shift and slightly bend knees") (2h)CL:5-claw(ball)"catch ball"

You could also use a classifier to show the ball in the air. You could use the CL:G handshape to show the ball is flying through the air toward the other person. You could also use the CL:5-claw handshape with the CL:B handshape on your non-dominant hand to show the ball bouncing on the ground or both hands with a CL:1 handshape held horizontally and moving away from you (like the opposite of the sign SIGN) to show the ball rolling on the ground.

ME CL:1(me)"stand here" MY BROTHER (dh)CL:1(me)/(nh)CL:V-curve(brother)"sit across from me" ME CL:5-claw(ball)"throw ball" CL:G(ball)"fly toward brother" MY BROTHER ("shift and slightly bend knees") (2h)CL:5-claw(ball)"catch ball"

The possibilities are truly endless!

Classifiers are a very important part of ASL. There isn't a sign for every English word and classifiers are able to fill those gaps and create more visual clarity.

It is difficult to fully explain classifiers in a book. The best way to practice and understand classifiers is to watch how signers tell stories and see them in action. I recommend looking for "classifier story" videos on the internet to see good examples of classifiers in action.

Verbs

You may have noticed that certain verbs are signed differently than others. There are four types of verbs in ASL: plain, directional, spatial, and classifier.

1. **Plain Verbs**
   With plain verbs, you need to specify the subject and object of the sentence, or they won't make any sense. (e.g. CAN)

2. **Directional Verbs**
   You can indicate the subject and object of the sentence by moving the directional verb between the subject and object of the sentence. The sign would start with the

subject and end with the object. These verbs can also specify the number of subjects or objects with a sweep, chop, or inward sweep movement. (e.g. he-GIVE-her)

Note: Directional verbs can also show a reciprocal action, like with the sign LOOK-AT-EACH-OTHER, where both hands are each directed from a referent and pointing toward each other, representing eyes looking at each other at the same time.

3. **Spatial/Locative Verbs**

    You need to specify the subject and object of the sentence with spatial verbs, but this verb is used to show location. For example, if I sign PUT-up, then that means something is being placed up high. The sign HURT can also be signed in different locations to show what part of the body is hurting. Another example would be the sign FLY. You can use directionality to show the location of you-FLY-there or she-FLY-here, etc.

Plain Verb   *Directional Verb*

Locative/Spatial Verb

4. **Classifier Verbs**

   As discussed earlier, classifiers can be used to show how something is doing an action. For example, using the CL:3 classifier for a vehicle, you can sign "CAR-DRIVE-DOWN-HILL" or "BICYCLE-DRIVE-BY" as part of a sentence.

"State of being" Verbs

ASL does not use "state of being" verbs. These are verbs like "am" in sentences like "I am a student."

You would sign the English sentence, "I am a student" as "ME STUDENT," "STUDENT ME," or even, "ME STUDENT ME" while nodding your head. These are all correct ASL sentences.

However, you can use the sign PAST/BEFORE for the past tense "was/were", the sign FUTURE/WILL for the future tense "will be", and the sign NOW/PRESENT/TODAY for the present tense "am/are/is".

You can also use the sign FINISH for present tense. For example, "ME FINISH BUY BOOK" or "ME BUY BOOK FINISH".

Temporal Aspect

Temporal aspect means showing how the verb is being done with relationship to time. You can inflect verbs to show if something is being done regularly, continually, repeatedly, or for an extended period of time.

You would use the following motions (and appropriate facial expressions) to show each:

- **Regularly:** Repeated straight line movement
- **Continually:** Repeated small circular movement
- **Repeatedly:** Repeated straight and circular movement
- **For an extended period:** Repeated large circular movement

For example, if you want to show that you study regularly, you would sign STUDY with a few straight movements toward your non-dominant hand with the appropriate facial expression. You would normally use this inflection if you are describing doing something frequently and its normal for you to do so.

_____"cs"

EVERY-WEEK ME *STUDY*"regularly"

If you want to show that you studied continually, you would sign STUDY with a repeated circular movement and the appropriate facial expression. You would normally use this inflection if you are describing doing something over a period of time, but the duration isn't too long for you.

_____"mm"

TODAY ME *STUDY*"continually"

If you want to show that you study repeatedly, you would sign STUDY with a straight movement toward your non-dominant hand, pause, and then sign a circular movement back to sign the straight movement again. You would sign this using the appropriate facial expression as well. You would normally use this inflection if you are describing doing something over and over again, and this is something you are getting a bit tired of.

_____"sta-sta-sta"

EVERY-WEEK ME *STUDY*"repeatedly"

If you want to show that you studied for a long period of time, you would sign STUDY with slow, long, circular movements with the appropriate facial expression. You would normally use this inflection if you are describing doing something for an extended period of time that usually wouldn't take that long (and you might not enjoy).

_____"cheeks puffed"

TODAY ME *STUDY*"for a long time"

For example, to indicate that you waited for a long time, you would sign WAIT more than once in a large, slow circular motion moving away from you while using the appropriate facial expression.

You would choose the inflection you use based on how *you* perceive the action. For example, one person might use the "long time" inflection for "wait for three hours" while someone else might use the "continually" inflection for that same sentence because three hours doesn't seem that long to that person.

These inflections can also be, and commonly are, used with adjectives such as SICK and WRONG to indicate inflections such as "sick for a long time" and "make mistakes regularly."

Time

Because there are no affixes in ASL to change the tense of verbs, time in ASL is communicated with time signs and inflections of time signs.

Time Signs

There are a couple easy rules to use when signing units of time.

You first need to know what "time signs" are. Here is a list to give you an idea of what signs are considered to be time signs:

- TIME
- MORNING
- AFTERNOON
- EVENING
- NIGHT
- LAST/PAST

- NOW
- MINUTE
- HOUR
- DAY
- WEEK
- MONTH

- YEAR
- TODAY
- TOMORROW
- YESTERDAY
- Etc.

Time signs follow certain movements. Signs that indicate the future move forward. Signs that indicate the past move backward. Signs that indicate the present are signed right in front of the body.

This image may help you understand the movements of time signs:

For example:

| *LAST WEEK* | *THIS WEEK* | *NEXT WEEK* |

Notice how the signs move forward, backward, or stay in front of the body depending on the time they represent? The same is true for signs such as YEAR-PAST, TWO-DAY-PAST, THREE-MONTH-FUTURE, etc.

Some signs use your non-dominant hand as a time referent instead of your body. For example, the signs POSTPONE and FROM-NOW-ON are non-symmetrical signs where one hand moves and your dominant hand moves forward away from your non-dominant hand.

Non-Manual Markers

There are a few non-manual markers that can be used to indicate time.

For example, the mouth movement "cs," where you clench your teeth and put your cheek to your shoulder, indicates recentness. This would be the difference between:

RECENT = "recent"

_____"cs"
RECENT = "very recent"

Another non-manual marker would be "cheeks puffed" where you close your mouth and puff out your cheeks to indicate a very distant time. Adding this marker to a sign can mean "a long time ago" or "a long time from now."

Numeral Incorporation

Numeral incorporation means incorporating a number into a sign. Just like how you can use numeral incorporation for age and money numbers, you can use numeral incorporation with time signs.

For example, instead of signing THREE before the sign WEEK for "three weeks," you would simply use the three-handshape as the handshape for your dominant hand while signing WEEK. Normally, you should only incorporate numbers up to the number 9. After that, you would sign the number first and then the sign.

You can use numeral incorporation for signs such as WEEK, HOUR, MINUTE, YEAR, MONTH, AND DAY. You can create signs such as TWO-YEARS, TWO-YEARS-PAST, TWO-YEARS-FUTURE, etc.

THREE WEEKS

Tense

In English, words are conjugated, words are added, or suffixes are added to indicate the past, present, and future. For example, "I <u>went</u> to the store," "<u>Last week</u> I played baseball," or "She notic<u>ed</u> him there."

In ASL, there is no sign for "went" or for the suffixes "-ing," "-ed," or "-s." Instead, signs like NEXT-WEEK, PAST-MONTH, NOW-AFTERNOON, or NEXT-MONTH are added to signed sentences to indicate tense.

For example, the sentences above would be signed, "YESTERDAY ME GO STORE," "LAST-WEEK ME PLAY BASEBALL," and after tense is created in context, "SHE NOTICE HIM."

You can also turn verbs like STUDY or LEARN into the present tense STUDYING or LEARNING by signing them more than once with a circular motion—as if they are current processes.

In ASL, the verbs always keep the same tense. The only change is the "time signs" that are added to the sentence or the conversation. Tense only needs to be established once in a signed conversation—you do not need to keep referring to the same tense in later sentences.

It is important to note that if you sign, "NOW-AFTERNOON ME EAT LUNCH," the interpretation depends on what time of the day it currently is. If it is morning, this sentence would mean, "This afternoon, I will eat lunch." If it is the evening, this sentence would mean, "Today I ate lunch."

Duration

You can indicate duration by inflecting time signs. For example, when you sign DAY, MORNING, or NIGHT with bigger signs, a longer movement, and a head tilt, you have signed, ALL-DAY, ALL-MORNING, or ALL-NIGHT.

DAY   *ALL-DAY*

You can also use this to create signs like ALL-WEEK, ALL-MONTH, and ALL-YEAR.

Regularity

To show something done on a habitual basis, you would use certain signs or modify the production of time signs.

For example, when you repeat the signs TOMORROW, WEEK, or MONTH, you create the words DAILY, WEEKLY, or MONTHLY. You can also use numeral incorporation with these signs to create phrases like "every four days," "every two weeks," "every three months," etc.

THREE-WEEKS

every-THREE-WEEKS

When you sign the days of the week with the normal handshape, but with a downward movement, you modify the meaning. For example, if you sign MONDAY with a straight downward movement instead of a small circular movement, this means EVERY-MONDAY.

MONDAY

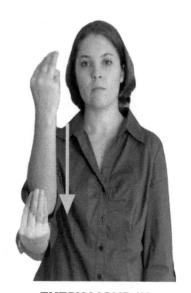

EVERY-MONDAY

The same works for signs like MORNING, AFTERNOON, and EVENING. If you sign these with the same handshape, but a sweep-to-the-right movement, it means EVERY-MORNING, EVERY-AFTERNOON, and EVERY-EVENING.

MORNING

EVERY MORNING

Moving Forward

In this section, you learned about ASL morphology and how to inflect signs to create different parts of sentences. In the next section, you will learn how to put these signs together to create accurate sentences in ASL.

6 American Sign Language
Syntax

In this section:
- **Word Order**
- **Sentence Types**
- **Negation**
- **Pronouns and Indexing**
- **Nouns**
- **Adjectives**
- **Auxiliary Verbs**
- **Prepositions**
- **Conjunctions**
- **Articles**

Syntax is the study of constructing sentences. Syntax also refers to the rules and principles of sentence structure.

In ASL, syntax is conveyed through word order and non-manual markers. This section can be confusing, so don't get discouraged if you don't understand the first time.

Word Order

ASL sentences follow a TOPIC-COMMENT structure. This is the same as the English "subject" "predicate" structure. However, instead of the topic always being the subject, the topic in ASL is whatever the comment is referring to. This can either be the subject of the sentence or the object.

The subject of a sentence is the person or object doing the action, the verb of a sentence is the action, and the object of a sentence is what is receiving the action. For example, in the sentence "The boy kicked the ball" the subject is "boy," the verb is "kicked," and the object is "ball."

There are a few different variations of word order in ASL depending on the vocabulary you are using and what you are trying to accomplish.

Word Order with Plain Verbs

When using plain verbs, ASL sentences can follow a variety of different word orders.

While English usually only follows Subject-Verb-Object word order, all of the following sentences are correct in ASL for the English sentence "Mother loves Father," when using plain verbs:

Subject-Verb-Object (SVO)	"MOTHER LOVE FATHER" "SHE LOVE HIM" "MOTHER LOVE HIM" "SHE LOVE FATHER"
Subject-Verb-Object-Subject (SVOS or SVO+Pronoun)	_____aff "MOTHER LOVE FATHER, MOTHER" ___aff "SHE LOVE HIM, SHE"
Object-Subject-Verb (OSV) ("Topicalization")	_____t "FATHER, MOTHER LOVE" ___t "HE, SHE LOVE"
Object-Subject-Verb-Subject (OSVS or OSV+Pronoun)	_____t _____aff "FATHER, MOTHER LOVE, MOTHER" ___t ___aff "HE, SHE LOVE, SHE"

You may also see these word orders used:

Verb-Object-Subject (VOS): "LOVE RICE ME"

___t
Object-Verb-Subject (OVS): "RICE, LOVE ME"

Object-Subject-Verb Word Order

In ASL, you can use either the subject or object as the TOPIC of a sentence. Using the subject as the topic is using an "active voice" and is in Subject-Verb-Object (SVO) word order. Using the object as the topic is using a "passive voice" and is in Object-Subject-Verb (OSV) word order.

Below are examples of each:

"Topic" is	Example	Topic	Comment	Literal Translation
Subject (SVO) "active voice"	GIRL KICK BALL	GIRL	KICK BALL	"The girl kicked the ball."
Object (OSV) "passive voice"	____t BALL, GIRL KICK	BALL	GIRL KICK	"The ball was kicked by the girl."

When the object is the topic of the sentence, this is called "topicalization." Topicalization is another kind of sentence structure that involves different non-manual markers than a simple SVO structure.

These sentences from the plain verb examples are topicalized sentences:

_____t
"FATHER, MOTHER LOVE" (OSV)
__t
"HE, SHE LOVE" (OSV)
_____t   _____aff
"FATHER, MOTHER LOVE, MOTHER" (OSVS)
__t   __aff
"HE, SHE LOVE, SHE" (OSV+Pronoun)

We will discuss topicalization non-manual markers later in this section.

Word Order without Objects

All of the following sentences are correct in ASL when signing a sentence without an object:

Subject-Verb (SV)	"MAN WORK" "HE WORK"
Subject-Verb-Subject (SVS or SV+Pronoun)	_aff "MAN WORK HE"
Verb-Pronoun (V+Pronoun)	_aff "WORK HE"

However, Verb-Subject (putting the verb before the subject of the sentence) would NOT be correct in ASL. For example, "WORK MAN" is not a correct ASL sentence.

Word Order with Directional Verbs

Directional verbs add additional meaning to sentences which, in turn, contributes to different word order variations. Because the subject and object of the sentence can be shown with just the movement of the directional verb, sometimes only the verb is signed with a certain directional movement.

All of the following sentences are correct in ASL when using directional verbs:

Subject-Verb-Object (SVO)	"me-GIVE-you BOOK" "he-GIVE-her BOOK"
Subject-Verb-Object-Subject (SVO or SVO+Pronoun)	_aff "HE he-GIVE-her BOOK, HE" ___aff "MAN he-GIVE-her BOOK, MAN" _aff "MAN he-GIVE-her BOOK, HE"
Object-Subject-Verb (OSV) ("Topicalization")	_____t "BOOK, he-GIVE-her"
Object-Subject-Verb-Subject (OSVS or OSV+Pronoun) ("Topicalization")	_____t _____aff "BOOK, he-GIVE-her, HE"

Time-Topic-Comment

When you talk about a past or future event in ASL, you would establish the time-frame before signing the rest of the sentence.

This creates a TIME-TOPIC-COMMENT structure. The same rules of word order for the TOPIC-COMMENT structure apply, only now a "time sign" is added to the beginning of the sentence.

Here are some examples:

Word Order	Sign Example	Literal Translation
Time-Subject-Verb-Object	LAST-WEEK GIRL KICK BALL	"The girl kicked the ball last week."
Time-Subject-Verb	YESTERDAY HE WALK	"He walked yesterday."
Time-Subject-Adjective	2-YEARS-AGO HE UGLY	"He was ugly 2 years ago."

Time signs are usually only signed at the beginning of sentences.

Sentence Types

There are a few different sentence types in ASL. These sentence types are not the same as word order. Word order shows the order in which you can sign your words. Sentence types show how to use word order along with non-manual markers to form certain types of sentences.

Questions

There are three types of questions used in ASL—wh-word questions, yes/no questions, and rhetorical questions. The only way to decipher between these questions in ASL is by the use of non-manual markers.

"Wh" Word Questions (whq)

Wh-word questions are questions that require more than a yes or no answer. These are normally questions that use the words who, what, when, where, why, or how. The wh-word is normally signed at the end of the question.

Non-Manual Markers:

- Lower your eyebrows
- Lean your head forward
- Hold the last sign in your sentence (usually the wh-word)

Wh-Word Question

Examples:

1.   __whq
   HE/SHE WHO? ("Who is he/she?")
2.   ___whq
   YOU LEARN SIGN WHERE? ("Where are you learning sign?")
3. _whq   __whq
   WHO YOUR TEACHER WHO? ("Who is your teacher?")

These common phrases are exceptions to the rule:

4. _____whq
   HOW YOU? ("How are you?")

5. _____whq
   WHAT TIME? ("What time is it?")

6. __whq
   TIME? ("What time is it?")

Yes/No Questions (y/n)

Yes/no questions are questions that only require a simple yes or no answer.

Non-Manual Markers:

- Raise your eyebrows
- Lean your head forward
- Hold the last sign in your sentence

Yes/No Question

Examples:

1. _____y/n
    DEAF YOU? ("Are you Deaf?")
2. _____y/n
    STUDENT HE/SHE? ("Is he/she a student?")
3. _____y/n
    YOU MARRIED YOU? ("Are you married?")

"Question Mark Wiggle"

A "question mark wiggle" is sometimes used to add doubt or incredulousness to a question. You would sign a question mark wiggle with a question like, "You really think she'll win that race?" and use a yes/no question facial expression. A question mark wiggle is signed by taking your index finger and flexing it a little into almost an x-handshape a few times at the end of a question.

Rhetorical Questions (rhq)

Rhetorical questions are not actual questions—a response is not expected. After asking the rhetorical question, you would immediately give the answer and other information. Rhetorical questions are used often with "why" questions in place of the word "because."

Non-Manual Markers:

- Make a statement using a neutral expression
- Ask a "wh" question with your eyebrows raised during the "wh" word
- Answer your own question with a neutral, affirmative, or negative expression

I...WHY?

EAT...NOT

Examples:

1.   __rhq _____neg
    ME HUNGRY, WHY? EAT LUNCH NOT.
    ("I'm hungry. Why? I didn't eat lunch")
    ("I'm hungry because I didn't eat lunch")

2.   __rhq _____aff
    THAT WOMAN, WHO? MY MOM.
    ("Who is that woman? My mom")
    ("That woman is my mom")

3.   __rhq _____aff
    ME PASS CLASS, HOW? ME STUDY.
    ("I passed the class. How? I studied")
    ("I passed the class because I studied")

Declarative Sentences

Declarative sentences are statements. These can be affirmative, negative, or neutral statements and each are recognized by the different non-manual markers that are used.

Affirmative Declarative Sentences

Non-Manual Marker:

- Nod your head while signing (use appropriate facial expression to show the degree or intensity of your affirmation)

Examples:

1. _____aff
   SHE DEAF SHE ("She is Deaf")
2. _____aff
   ME HUNGRY ("I'm hungry")
3. _____aff
   ME WASH CAR FINISH ("I washed the car")

Negative Declarative Sentences

Non-Manual Markers:

- Shake your head
- Scrunch up your face
- Frown
- Use appropriate facial expression to show the degree or intensity of your negation

Examples:

1. _____neg
   ME GO CAN'T ("I can't go")
2. _____neg
   ME HUNGRY ("I'm not hungry")
3. _____neg
   ME WASH CAR NOT-YET FINISH ("I'm not finished washing the car")
4. _____neg
   ME NOT HUNGRY ("I'm not hungry")
5. _____neg
   ME HAVE NONE CHILDREN ("I have no children")

6. _____neg
   ME NOT HAVE TIME ("I don't have time")

Neutral Declarative Sentences

Non-Manual Marker:

- Neutral head position (no shaking or nodding)

Examples:

1. ME GO HOME ("I'm going home")
2. MY SISTER WANT GO STORE ("My sister wants to go to the store")
3. ME EAT FINISH ("I'm done eating")

Conditional Sentences (cond)

Conditional sentences follow an if/then structure where the non-manual markers for the "if" part of the sentence differ from the ones for the "then" part of the sentence.

The signs SUPPOSE, IF, and #IF are also commonly used with the conditional facial expressions to mark the beginning of conditional statements.

Non-Manual Markers:

- Raise your eyebrows during the "if" part of the sentence
- Then make a question or declarative statement for the "then" part of the sentence

TODAY RAIN,   *GAME CANCEL.*

Examples:

1. _____cond _____aff
   TODAY RAIN, GAME CANCEL.
   ("If it rains today, the game will be cancelled")

2. _____cond _____y/n
   TODAY RAIN, YOU LEAVE YOU?
   ("If it rains today, are you going to leave?")

3. _____cond ___whq ____whq
   TODAY RAIN, WHERE YOU GO WHERE?
   ("If it rains today, where will you go?")

4. _____cond ____aff
   MILK CHEAP, ME BUY.
   ("If the milk is cheap, I will buy it")

5. ____cond _____aff
   ME SICK, LEAVE EARLY.
   ("If I'm sick, I will leave early")

Topicalization (t)

When you use the "object" part of the sentence as the topic of the sentence (OSV word order), this is called topicalization. The facial expression used for the "object" part of the sentence differs from the rest of the sentence. This creates a "passive voice" instead of the "active voice" that is used with SVO structure.

Topicalized Statements

Non-Manual Markers:

- Raise your eyebrows for the "topic" part of the sentence
- Then make a neutral, affirmative, or negative declarative statement for the "comment" part of the sentence

Examples:

1. _____t _____aff
   MY DAD, THAT MAN. ("That man is my dad")

2. _____t _____aff
   FATHER, MOTHER LOVE. ("Mother loves father")

3. _____t   ___"pah"
   THAT KEY, ME FINALLY FIND
   ("I finally found that key")

4. _____t _____aff
   THAT DRAWING, ME DRAW. ("I drew that drawing")

Topicalized "Wh" Question

Non-Manual Markers:

- Raise your eyebrows for the "topic" part of the sentence
- Then lower your eyebrows to ask the "Wh" question

...GIRL, WHO?

Examples:

1. _____t __whq
   THAT GIRL, WHO?
   ("Who is that girl?")

2. _____t __whq
   THAT DRAWING, WHAT?
   ("What is that a drawing of?")

3. _____t __whq
   TWO-OF-US LEAVE EARLY, HOW?
   ("How are we going to leave early?")

Negation

To **form a negative**, you can:

- Sign NOT before the word.

- Shake your head while signing the word.

- Use reversal of orientation for some signs.

- Frown while signing the word.

Non-manual markers are a very important part of negation. For example, if you sign, "ME don't-LIKE HAMBURGER," a different facial expression can change the meaning to: "I really dislike hamburgers."

Reversal of Orientation

Reversal of orientation is one way to form a negative. When you reverse your palm orientation of some signs, you can express the opposite of the meaning of the original sign.

For example, you can change the sign for WANT to don't-WANT by signing WANT then reversing your palm orientation so your palms are facing downward while using a negative facial expression.

WANT

DON'T-WANT

You can use reversal of orientation for the signs WANT, KNOW, and LIKE to mean don't-WANT, don't-KNOW, or don't-LIKE.

Pronouns and Indexing

Indexing is when you set up a point to refer to a person or object that is or is not present in the signing area. This is also known as referencing or creating referents.

If the person or object is present, you can just point at him, her, or it to mean HE/HIM, SHE/HER, or IT.

If the person or object is not present, you would first need to identify the person or object. Then, you can "index" the person or object to a point in space. Once you have set up this referent, you can refer back to that same point every time you want to talk about that person or object.

To refer to referents, you would use these types of signs:

- Personal Pronouns
- Possessive Pronouns
- Directional Verbs

For example, if you are talking about Bill and Suzy, you can sign Bill's name and point to your left. Then, you can sign Suzy's name and point to your right. When continuing your dialogue about Bill and Suzy, you would then point to your left or right whenever you refer to them (you would no longer need to spell out their names).

Indexing on your non-dominant hand

You can also use your non-dominant hand as a way to index and talk about your friends or family.

For example, when you are talking about your siblings, you can index them on your non-dominant hand by pointing to different fingers for each sibling, starting with your thumb for your oldest sibling and working your way down to your last finger for the youngest.

Example

Personal Pronouns

In ASL, personal pronouns are signed by pointing with your index finger toward a person, object, or referent. A referent is used when a person or object is not present.

Here are the signs used for personal pronouns:

I/ME = point at yourself, touching your chest

YOU = point at the person you are talking to

HE/SHE/IT = point to the person or object you are talking about (or to the spot you are using to reference the person or object)

THOSE/THEY/THEM = point to the group or point and sweep your hand to the side toward the people you are referencing (to the right or left)

THIS = point to a certain object or to the spot you are referencing

THESE = point slightly downward and sweep your hand toward the objects you are referencing (to the right or left)

WE/US = use your index finger starting on your chest near the shoulder of your dominant hand (palm facing in) and flip it in a half circle to near the shoulder of your non-dominant hand (palm facing in)

ALL-OF-YOU = point and sweep your hand in front of you toward the people you are referencing

TWO-OF-YOU = use the k-handshape with your palm up and point to the "you" person (in front of you) and the other person you are referencing with a side-to-side shaking movement

TWO-OF-THEM = use the k-handshape with your palm up and point to the two people you are referencing with a side-to-side shaking movement

TWO-OF-US = use the k-handshape and point to yourself with your middle finger and point to the "you" person (in front of you) with your index finger with a back-and-forth shaking movement

THREE-OF-YOU = use the 3-handshape with your palm up and make a horizontal circle pointing to the "you" person (in front of you) and the other two people you are referencing

THREE-OF-THEM = use the 3-handshape with your palm up and make a horizontal circle pointing to the three people you are referencing

THREE-OF-US = use the 3-handshape with your palm up and make a horizontal circle close to your body, pointing at yourself, the "you" person (in front of you), and the other person you are referencing

Possessive Pronouns

In ASL, personal pronouns can indicate possession simply by changing your handshape from an index finger to a flat hand. The palm of your flat hand would be pointing toward the person or object.

For example, to sign YOUR, you would sign YOU with a flat hand, fingertips up, and your palm facing toward the person.

Here are the possession signs:

MY/MINE = flat hand on your chest

YOUR/YOURS = flat hand toward the "you" person (in front of you)

HIS/HER/HERS/ITS = flat hand toward the person or object

OUR/OURS = flat hand starting on your chest near the shoulder of your dominant hand (palm facing in) and flipping it in a half-circle to near the shoulder of your non-dominant hand (palm facing in)

THEIR/THEIRS = flat hand making a sweeping motion toward the people you are referring to

Instead of indexing, you can also indicate possession by using the sign "HAVE." For example, you can sign "ME HAVE BROTHER THREE" to mean "I have three brothers."

Another way you can show possession is the order of the words you sign. For example, if you sign "MY BROTHER FRIEND SICK," the order of your words ("friend" right after "brother") means that the friend is your brother's. Of course, if you were to use indexing, it would be best to sign "MY BROTHER, HIS FRIEND SICK".

Another way of showing possession is by using the "'s" sign. The "'s" is signed by taking the s-handshape and twisting your wrist to create a downward circle. However, this sign is normally only used in ASL when fingerspelling a title that has an "'s" in it, like "Fernando's Restaurant".

Directional Verbs

Directional verbs are also used for referring to referents. Directional verbs can show "who did what to whom" just by the movement between referents. This movement indicates the subject and the object of the verb in the sentence.

For example, if I sign GIVE starting near my body and move it in your direction, then I would have signed the directional verb "me-GIVE-you."

I can also start the sign GIVE away from my body (toward you) and then move it toward me and end near my body to sign "you-GIVE-me."

If I move the sign GIVE from starting toward you out to my left or my right, I would be signing "you-GIVE-him" or "you-GIVE-her."

I can also start GIVE toward my left and move it toward my right to sign "he/she-GIVE-him/her."

you-GIVE-me

you-GIVE-him/her

me-GIVE-you

he/she-GIVE-him/her

This directionality can be used with many signs for verbs, but not all of them. Here are some examples of verbs with which you can use directionality: GIVE, HELP, SHOW, HATE, TEACH, HIT, say-NO-to, ASK, SEE, PAY, INVITE, SEND, BITE, BORROW, INFORM, and TAKE. However, you cannot use directionality with signs such as WANT and LOVE. You would have to sign "HE LOVE HER" or "SHE WANT SODA."

An interesting directional verb is the sign MEET. I can sign "I meet you" just by facing the back of my non-dominant hand toward you and the back of my dominant hand toward me when I bring my hands together to form the sign MEET.

me-MEET-you

Plural Directional Verbs

To use a directional verb for something that is being done to multiple people, you would use a sweep, chop, or inward sweep motion. Your body will also slightly shift along with these movements.

For example, to give a book to a group in general, you would just sweep the sign GIVE, starting near your body, horizontally from your left to your right. You can also do this sign simultaneously with both hands.

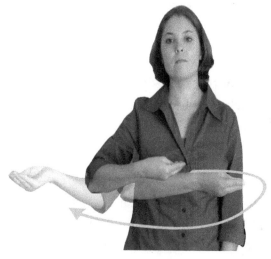

GIVE(to group)

To give a book to a few or several individuals, you would sign short "me-GIVE-you" motions strung together while sweeping your hand horizontally from the left to the right.

GIVE(to few)

You can also sign GIVE(to few) or GIVE(to several) with both hands alternating the me-GIVE-you motions.

To give a book to only a certain number of people, you would sign that number of "me-GIVE-you" motions to those referents in space.

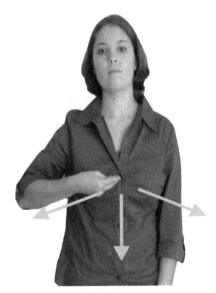

GIVE(to three)

Nouns

Generally, a noun represents a person, place, thing, or idea. In ASL sentences, nouns can be combined with adjectives and pronouns.

Here are some examples of nouns in ASL sentences:

_____t
"**MAN,** HE WORK"

_____t
"**WOMAN,** SHE NICE"

_____t
"**MAN,** HE **HOME**"

_____aff
"HE **MAN**"

Pluralization

In English, nouns become plural with the "-s" or "-es" suffix. However, ASL does not have a sign for these English suffixes and it's not always necessary.

For example, for the sentence, "How many cars do you have?" you would sign "HOW-MANY CAR YOU HAVE YOU?" The plural doesn't matter.

However, if you want to emphasize a plural for sentences like, "I have two cars," you have a few different options:

- **Use repetition.** For example, you would sign the word CANCEL a couple times to mean "cancellations."

- **Add a number to the sign.** For example, signing "MAN FIVE" to mean "five men."

- **Use numeral incorporation.** For example, signing WEEK with the 2-handshape to mean "two weeks." You can also do this for signs like MONTH, YEAR, HOUR, etc.

- **Add a quantifier sign like FEW, MANY, SOME, BOTH, etc.** For example, signing "MAN MANY" to mean "many men."

- **Add a plural classifier.** For example, signing MAN then the classifier for HORDES-OF to mean "hordes of men."

- **Repeat the verb.** For example, signing "CLOTHES ME BUY, (shift) BUY, (shift) BUY" to mean "I bought many clothes."

- **Use plural pronouns.** For example, WE, ALL-OF-YOU, THEY, etc.

Adjectives

Adjectives are words that describe nouns. In ASL, they can be placed before or after a noun, or both and can also be inflected with facial expression.

Here are some examples of adjectives in ASL sentences:

"WE EAT **DELICIOUS** SOUP"
"WE EAT SOUP **DELICIOUS**"
"WE EAT **DELICIOUS** SOUP **DELICIOUS**" (for emphasis)

If there is more than one adjective, sign all of them after the noun:

"WE EAT SOUP **HOT, DELICIOUS**"
"THAT MOVIE **CUTE, FUNNY**. ME ENJOY."

Auxiliary Verbs

Auxiliary verbs like WILL, CAN, SHOULD, NEED-TO, MUST, WOULD, MIGHT, COULD, etc. can be used before or after the verb in an ASL sentence. For example:

"YOU **NEED** BUY BOOK"
"YOU BUY BOOK **NEED**"
"YOU **NEED** BUY BOOK **NEED**" (for emphasis)

Prepositions

Prepositions show how a noun and a predicate relate. In English, words like "before", "behind", "inside", and "above" are prepositions.

Prepositions in ASL are normally shown with classifiers and indexing which were discussed earlier.

For example, you could sign "The shoes are under the bed" with "BED CL:B"here", SHOES CL:B"under bed"" using classifiers.

However, there are some signs for prepositions in ASL: NEXT-TO, UNDER, IN, OUTSIDE, ON, NEAR, etc.

For example:

```
_____t                          __aff
```
YOUR SHOES, BED IT(index bed) UNDER IT(index bed)

Conjunctions

The only conjunctions that have a sign in ASL are BUT and #OR. To indicate the other conjunctions, there are certain grammatical rules that are used in ASL.

Instead of using the word "and" for lists, ASL uses the non-dominant hand. You would first show the length of the list with your non-dominant hand (thumb pointing upward) and then explain the items on the list after pointing to the finger on your non-dominant hand that represents that item. The handshapes for the numbers on your list are the same as normal cardinal numbers.

For example, if you had a grocery list you would sign, "ME NEED (nh)FOUR-LIST, FIRST-OF-FOUR-LIST ORANGES, SECOND-OF-FOUR-LIST CHEESE, THIRD-OF-FOUR-LIST MILK, FOURTH-OF-FOUR-LIST WATER." You can also sign the items while still holding up your non-dominant hand.

FIRST-OF-FOUR-LIST ORANGES

Instead of using the word "or," you can use a shoulder twist. You would shift your shoulders slightly to the left for the first part and then shift your shoulders slightly to the right for the second part. You can then follow this with a sign like WHICH in the neutral position to ask which you should choose.

For example, if you can't decide which to do first, you would sign "FIRST ME GO STORE [shoulder twist] GO HOME, WHICH?"

STORE...HOME...WHICH?

You can also sign "FIRST ME GO STORE #OR HOME, WHICH?"

An example of using the sign BUT is the sentence, "GREEN ME WANT, BUT YELLOW don't-WANT." In English, this means, "I want green, but I don't want yellow."

Articles

In ASL, there are no separate signs for articles (e.g. "a," "an," and "the"). They are not necessary. Instead, ASL uses non-manual markers and indexing and incorporates them into other signs.

For example, consider the sentence "I am a teacher." You would simply sign "ME TEACHER" while nodding your head. This way, the signs "am" and "a" are incorporated into the sentence with the non-manual head nod.

Another example would be the sentence, "The boy ran." You would sign, "BOY RUN." The word "the" is already incorporated.

Moving Forward

In this section, you learned about ASL syntax and how to create accurate sentences in ASL. This completes the sections of ASL grammar. Make sure to check out the Translation Study Sheet and the Glossary of Terms. They are sure to be of help to you on your ASL journey.

Final Chapter

Congratulations!

Just by reading this book, you have learned the essentials of ASL grammar. You have saved yourself a lot of time and now know how to accurately sign in American Sign Language!

Many ASL students go *years* without learning how to correctly sign using ASL grammar. Too many signers fall back into English structure because they haven't fully learned the ASL grammar rules.

But you're different! You are now starting out on the right foot, prepared with the knowledge of ASL grammar. Even if you have difficulty adjusting in the beginning, you are armed with the right information to improve your skills and move toward truly signing in American Sign Language.

Now go out there and sign! ☺

Signed always,

Michelle Jay

Translation Study Sheet

English	ASL
Lexicalized Fingerspelling	
"I will give it back when I'm finished."	_____t ___aff ME FINISH, give-#BACK WILL
"Ouch, that *hurt*!"	WOW *#HURT!*
State Abbreviations	
"We're going to visit Michigan next year."	NEXT-YEAR TWO-OF-US VISIT fs- ___aff MI WILL
Numbers	
"I have two brothers."	ME HAVE BROTHER TWO
"I just finished my sixth book."	ME RECENTLY FINISH BOOK SIXTH
"Can I borrow five dolllars?"	_____y/n PLEASE you-LEND-me 5-DOLLARS?
"I am 25 years old."	_____aff ME AGE-25
"It's 12 o'clock"	NOW TIME 12
Name Signs	
"My name is Amber."	MY NAME fs-AMBER (name sign)"tap A on shoulder"

"No" Signs

"No, I don't like pickles."

_____neg
NO ME don't-LIKE PICKLES

"I am not driving."

_____neg
ME DRIVE NOT

"I have no children."

_____neg
ME HAVE CHILDREN NONE

Signs without an English Translation

"Have you ever been to New York?"

_____y/n
FINISH-TOUCH NEW-YORK YOU?

"I usually brush my teeth in the morning."

MORNING ME TEND-TO BRUSH-TEETH

"Thomas Hopkins Gallaudet has a very good reputation."

_____t _____
GALLAUDET(name sign), NAME-
____aff
SHINE

"Would it be ok if I interrupt?"

_____y/n
don't-MIND ME INTERRUPT?

"This morning I got up, ate breakfast, brushed my teeth, then drove to school."

MORNING ME GET-UP, EAT BREAKFAST
FINISH, BRUSH-TEETH FINISH, DRIVE
SCHOOL

"Are you done with your homework?"

_____y/n
HOMEWORK FINISH YOU?

"She is much better now that she is done with surgery."

_____t
SURGERY FINISH, SHE BETTER NOW

"I am not done washing the car."

_____neg
ME NOT-YET FINISH WASH CAR

Facial Expressions

"I'm very happy."

        _____aff
ME *HAPPY*

"Where are you going?"

___whq   ___whq
WHERE YOU GO WHERE?

"Are you going home?"

_____y/n
YOU GO HOME YOU?

Mouth Movements

"I drank a large cup of soda."

      __"cha"
ME FINISH DRINK LARGE SODA

"I finally finished my term paper!"

_____t   ___"pah"
TERM PAPER, ME FINALLY FINISH

"I finished washing the car."

  __"fsh"
ME FINISH WASH-CAR

"The chocolate melted all over the place."

   _"thh"
CHOCOLATE MELT

"I broke the phone."

  __"bro"
ME BROKE PHONE

"I finished very recently."

_____"cs"
ME RECENT FINISH

"She doesn't pay attention when she drives."

 __"th"
SHE DRIVE

"Yesterday, I was just walking along like normal."

  _"mm"
YESTERDAY ME WALK

"I saw a huge crowd of people."

   "cheeks
_____puffed"
ME SEE PEOPLE HORDES-OF

"She is very thin."

"lips
_pursed"
SHE THIN

"She struggled a lot with math."

_____t   _"sta-sta-sta"
MATH, SHE STRUGGLE++

Role Shifting

"Mom likes milk and Dad likes water."

(shift right) MOM LIKE MILK (shift left) DAD LIKE WATER

"I threw the ball and my brother caught it."

ME CL:5-claw(throw ball) MY BROTHER (shift) CL:5-claw(catch ball)

Inflection (adverbs)

"She walks very slow."

SHE *WALK*"slow"

"She is very beautiful."

SHE *BEAUTIFUL*!

"I want a very large soda."

_"cha"
ME WANT LARGE SODA

Numeral Incorporation

"I went to the beach three weeks ago."

THREE-WEEKS-AGO ME GO BEACH

"That boring speech lasted three long hours!"

SPEECH BORING *THREE-HOURS CONTINUE++*

Classifiers

"The car drove by five minutes ago."

FIVE-MINUTES PAST CAR CL:3(car)"drive by" FINISH

"I threw the ball and my brother caught it."

ME CL:5-claw(throw ball) MY BROTHER (shift) CL:5-claw(catch ball)

"That line is so long!"

(2h)CL:4(people in line)"long line"

"Today, two cars crashed into each other."	TODAY TWO CAR (dh)CL:3(car)/(nh) CL:3(car)"drive toward each other and crash"
"While I was walking today, I tripped and fell over a thin pole laying in the middle of the walkway."	TODAY ME WALK CL:1(me)"walk forward" WRONG HAPPEN (2h) CL:F(thin pole) P-O-L-E (nh)CL:1(pole on ground)/ME (dh)CL:V-inv(me)"trip and fall"
"While standing, I threw the ball to my brother who was sitting and he caught it."	ME CL:1(me)"stand here" MY BROTHER (dh)CL:1(me)/(nh)CL:V-curve(brother)"sit across from me" ME CL:5-claw(ball)"throw ball" MY BROTHER ("shift and slightly bend knees") (2h)CL:5-claw(ball)"catch ball"

Verbs

"I love my husband"	_aff ME LOVE MY HUSBAND ME
"I gave her the book"	me-GIVE-her BOOK FINISH
"Please maintain eye contact with me when I'm signing."	_____t ME SIGN, PLEASE you/me-LOOK-AT-each-other
"My leg hurts."	_aff HURT(leg) ME
"I flew to New York."	ME me-FLY-TO-there NEW-YORK FINISH
"I am a student."	_aff ME STUDENT ME
"I bought the book."	ME BUY BOOK FINISH

Temporal Aspect

125

"I regularly study every week."

_____ "cs"
EVERY-WEEK ME *STUDY* "regularly"

"I studied for a little while today."

_____ "mm"
TODAY ME *STUDY* "continually"

"I'm sick of studying so much every week."

_____ "sta-sta-sta"
EVERY-WEEK ME *STUDY* "repeatedly".
ME SICK-OF.

"Today I studied for a very long time."

_____ "cheeks puffed"
TODAY ME *STUDY* "for a long time"

Time

"I went to the store yesterday."

YESTERDAY ME GO STORE

"Last week I played baseball."

LAST-WEEK ME PLAY BASEBALL

Time - Regularity

"I wash my car every two weeks."

every-TWO-WEEKS ME TEND-TO WASH CAR

"I go to work every Monday."

every-MONDAY ME GO WORK

"I brush my teeth every morning."

every-MORNING ME TEND-TO BRUSH-TEETH

Time - Duration

"I exercised all morning."

ALL-MORNING ME EXERCISE

Plural Directional Verbs

"I gave everyone a packet."

_____ t
PACKET, ME GIVE "all" FINISH

"I gave the three of them a packet." _____t
PACKET, ME GIVE++ FINISH

Plain Verbs

"Mother loves Father." MOTHER LOVE FATHER

_aff
MOTHER LOVE FATHER, SHE

_____t
FATHER, MOTHER LOVE

_____t _____aff
FATHER, MOTHER LOVE, MOTHER

"I love rice." LOVE RICE ME

____t
RICE, LOVE ME

Sentences with no object

"He is stupid." MAN WORK
HE WORK

_aff
MAN WORK, HE

_aff
WORK, HE

Directional Verbs

"I gave you the book." me-GIVE-you BOOK

"He gave her the book." he-GIVE-her BOOK

_aff
HE he-GIVE-her BOOK, HE

__aff
MAN he-GIVE-her BOOK, HE

_____t __aff
BOOK, he-GIVE-her, HE

TIME-TOPIC-COMMENT

"The girl kicked the ball last week."	LAST-WEEK GIRL KICK BALL
"He walked yesterday."	YESTERDAY HE WALK
"He was ugly 2 years ago."	2-YEARS-AGO HE UGLY

Wh-Word Questions

"Who is he/she?"

          _whq
HE/SHE WHO?

"Where are you learning sign?"

          ___whq
YOU LEARN SIGN WHERE?

"Who is your teacher?"

_whq   _whq
WHO YOUR TEACHER WHO?

"How are you?"

      _____whq
HOW YOU?

"What time is it?"

      _____whq
WHAT TIME?

"What time is it?"

_whq
TIME?

Yes/No Questions

"Are you Deaf?"

      _____y/n
DEAF YOU?

"Is he/she a student?"

      _____y/n
STUDENT HE/SHE?

"Are you married?"

      _____y/n
YOU MARRIED YOU?

"You really think she'll win?"

      _____y/n
YOU THINK SHE WIN WILL "QMW"

Rhetorical Questions

"I'm hungry because I didn't eat lunch"

         _rhq   _____neg
ME HUNGRY, WHY? EAT LUNCH NOT.

"That woman is my mom"

         _rhq
THAT WOMAN, WHO? MY MOM.

"I passed the class because I studied"

         _rhq
ME PASS CLASS, HOW? I STUDY.

Affirmative Declarative Sentences

"She is Deaf"

      _____aff
SHE DEAF SHE

"I'm hungry"

      _____aff
ME HUNGRY

"I washed the car"

      _____aff
ME WASH CAR FINISH

Negative Declarative Sentences

"I can't go"

      _____neg
ME GO CAN'T

"I'm not hungry"

      _____neg
ME HUNGRY

"I'm not finished washing the car"

      _____neg
ME WASH CAR NOT-YET FINISH

"I'm not hungry"

      _____neg
ME NOT HUNGRY

"I have no children"

      _neg
ME HAVE NONE CHILDREN

"I don't have time"

_____neg
ME NOT HAVE TIME

Conditional Sentences

"If it rains today, the game will be cancelled"

_____cond _____aff
TODAY RAIN, GAME CANCEL.

"If it rains today, are you going to leave?"

_____cond _____y/n
TODAY RAIN, YOU LEAVE YOU?

"If it rains today, where will you go?"

_____cond _____whq
TODAY RAIN, WHERE YOU GO
____whq
WHERE?

"If the milk is cheap, I will buy it"

_____cond ____aff
MILK CHEAP, ME BUY.

"If I'm sick, I will leave early"

____cond _____aff
ME SICK, LEAVE EARLY.

Topicalized Statements

"That man is my dad"

_____t _____aff
MY DAD, THAT MAN.

"Mother loves father"

_____t _____aff
FATHER, MOTHER LOVE.

"I drew that drawing"

_____t _____aff
THAT DRAWING, ME DRAW.

Topicalized Wh Questions

"Who is that girl?"

_____t _whq
THAT GIRL, WHO?

"What is that a drawing of?"

_____t __whq
THAT DRAWING, WHAT?

"How are we going to leave early?"   _____t _whq
TWO-OF-US LEAVE EARLY, HOW?

Pronouns and Indexing

"I have two brothers and two sisters. I am the middle child."

ME HAVE BROTHER TWO (shift) SISTER TWO. (nh)FIVE-LIST, THIRD-OF-FIVE-LIST ME

"The three of us are going to New York."

THREE-OF-US TOUCH NEW-YORK WILL

"What is your name?"

        __whq
YOUR NAME WHAT?

"I have three brothers."   ME HAVE BROTHER THREE

"My brother's friend is sick."   MY BROTHER FRIEND SICK

"Nice to meet you."

_____aff
NICE me-MEET-you

Identifying People

"Do you see that woman with the red hair?"

_____

SEE THAT WOMAN "over there"
_____y/n
HAIR RED?

"You know Kary? She graduated college."

_____whq/t _____
KNOW K-A-R-Y, SHE GRADUATE
_____aff
COLLEGE

Pluralization

"How many cars do you have?"

_____whq
HOW-MANY CAR YOU HAVE YOU?

"We had a lot of cancellations."   WE HAVE MANY CANCEL++

"It's a large crowd of people." PEOPLE CL:5-claw(people)"hordes-of"

Adjectives

"We ate delicious soup." WE EAT DELICIOUS SOUP

WE EAT SOUP DELICIOUS

"We ate hot, delicious soup." WE EAT SOUP HOT, DELICIOUS

"I enjoyed that cute and funny movie." THAT MOVIE CUTE, FUNNY. ME ENJOY.

Auxiliary Verbs

"You need to buy the book." YOU NEED BUY BOOK

YOU BUY BOOK NEED

YOU NEED BUY BOOK NEED

Prepositions

"The shoes are under the bed" BED CL:B"here", SHOES CL:B"under bed"

"Your shoes are under the bed"
_____t
YOUR SHOES, BED IT(index bed)
    _aff
UNDER IT(index bed)

Conjunctions

"I need oranges, cheese, milk, and water." ME NEED (nh)FOUR-LIST, FIRST-OF-FOUR-LIST ORANGES, SECOND-OF-FOUR-LIST CHEESE, THIRD-OF-FOUR-LIST MILK, FOURTH-OF-FOUR-LIST WATER.

"Should I go to the store or home first?"
_____
FIRST ME GO STORE (shift) GO
_____whq
HOME, WHICH?

"Should I go to the store or home first?"

_____
FIRST ME GO STORE #OR HOME,
____whq
WHICH?

"I want green, but I don't want yellow."

GREEN ME WANT, BUT YELLOW
_____neg
don't-WANT

Articles

"I am a teacher."

_____aff
ME TEACHER

"The boy ran."

_____aff
BOY RUN

Glossary

A

Abbreviation: An abbreviation is a shortened form of a word or phrase. For example, in ASL, fingerspelling J-A-N means "January."

ABCOS15: The handshapes "ABCOS15" are the handshapes that are formed by your non-dominant hand while signing. When signing a two-handed sign where one hand moves, these are the handshapes your non-dominant hand uses as a stationary base for your moving dominant hand. For example, the sign HELP is made by supporting your dominant hand with the B handshape of your non-dominant hand.

Acronym: An acronym is a word formed from the first letters of words in a phrase. For example, the acronym for American Sign Language is ASL.

Active voice: Active voice in a sentence is used to show that the subject is the one performing the action. An example in ASL would be the signed sentence "GIRL KICK BALL." In English, this is translated into "The girl kicked the ball."

Adjective: An adjective is a word that describes a noun or pronoun. For example, in the sentence "The brown dog ran home," the word "brown" is an adjective. In ASL, adjectives can be signed before or after the noun, or both.

Adverb: An adverb is a word that modifies an adjective, verb, or another adverb to indicate time, place, manner, cause, or intensity. For example, English words like "quickly," "boldly," and "slowly" are adverbs. In ASL, there are no separate signs for adverbs; they are created by adding inflection to a sign. Inflection can include varying the intensity or speed of signing or incorporating facial expression. For example, the sign for WALK can be made quickly or slowly to indicate how the person is walking.

Affix: An affix is an element of grammar, such as a prefix or suffix, which is added to a word to form a new word. For example, you can add the suffix "-ed" to the word "want" to form the word "wanted." In ASL, there are no signs for affixes like "-en," "im-," "-ly," etc. to change the meaning of words. Instead, ASL uses non-manual markers, changes in parameters, and other signs to indicate tense, degree, intensity, plurality, aspect, and more.

American Manual Alphabet: The American Manual Alphabet is the twenty-six handshapes that represent the letters of the American alphabet.

American Sign Language (ASL): American Sign Language is the natural language of around 500,000 deaf people in the U.S. and Canada.

Amount Classifiers: These are classifiers where the handshapes show the increase or decrease in the amount or volume of something. For example, CL:B-bent(liquid level decreasing), etc.

Arbitrary name sign: An arbitrary name sign uses the first letter of the person's name.

Arbitrary sign: An arbitrary sign is a sign that doesn't look like the word it is representing.

Articles: With regard to grammar, an article is used to indicate nouns. For example, in English, the words "the," "a," and "an" are articles. In ASL, there are no separate signs for articles. They are not necessary. Instead, ASL uses non-manual markers and indexing and incorporates them into other signs. For example, consider the sentence "I am a teacher." You would simply sign "ME TEACHER" while nodding your head. This way, the signs "am" and "a" are incorporated into the sentence with the non-manual head nod.

ASL: *see* American Sign Language

Aspect: Grammatical aspect of a verb is the "tense" of the verb. In ASL, this is produced by changing parameters of the verb. Some changes you can apply include the addition of time signs and repetition. For example, the sign NEXT-WEEK can be added to a signed sentence to indicate the tense.

Assimilation: In ASL, assimilation is when a sign adopts the handshape, movement, location, or palm orientation of another sign. For example, many compound signs have developed over time and now look like one sign instead of two separate ones. For example, the sign BROTHER is made by signing BOY+SAME where BOY now has only one movement and SAME has a different palm orientation that looks more like the sign CORRECT.

Auxiliary Verbs: Auxiliary verbs like WILL, CAN, SHOULD, NEED-TO, MUST, WOULD, MIGHT, COULD, etc. can be used before or after the verb in an ASL sentence.

B

Body Classifiers: These are classifiers where the handshape shows a part of your body doing an action. For example, CL:V(look around), (2h)CL:G(big smile), (2h)CL:B(foot stumble), etc.

Body language: Body language is one of the many non-manual markers. One way you can use body language in ASL is with role shifting.

Body Shift: A body shift is used while signing to represent two or more characters in a conversation or signed story. This is done by shifting your upper torso to your left or right.

C

Cardinal Numbers: Cardinal numbers are the numbers used for counting.

Classifiers: Classifiers are signs used to describe the size and shape of an object (or person). They can be used to represent the object itself or the way the object moves or relates to other objects (or people). An example of a classifier is using the 3-handshape to represent a car as it drives through the mountains.

Classifier Verbs: Classifiers can be used to show how something is doing an action. For example, using the CL:3 classifier for a vehicle, you can sign "CAR-DRIVE-DOWN-HILL" or "BICYCLE-DRIVE-BY" as part of a sentence.

COMMENT: COMMENT refers to the COMMENT part of the TOPIC-COMMENT sentence structure of ASL syntax. For example, in the ASL sentence, "HOME ME GO," "ME GO" is the COMMENT.

Compound sign: A compound sign is a sign made by combining two or more signs. For example, the sign REMEMBER is a combination of the signs KNOW and CONTINUE.

Cond: *see* Conditional sentences

Conditional sentences (cond): In ASL, conditional sentences are sentences that follow an if/then structure where the facial expressions for the "if" part of the sentence are specific and different from the facial expressions for the "then" part of the sentence. For example, in ASL, the sentence, "TODAY RAIN, GAME CANCEL" is a conditional sentence. This sentence translates into "If it rains today, the game will be cancelled" in English.

Conjugate: To conjugate means to inflect a verb and can indicate tense. For example, the sentence, "I went to the store," uses the word "went" instead of the word "go" to indicate tense.

Conjunctions: Conjunctions are words that connect words, phrases, and sentences. For example, in English, the words "and," "but," "because," and "however" are all conjunctions. The only conjunctions that have a sign in ASL are BUT and #OR. To indicate the other conjunctions, there are certain grammatical rules that are used in ASL.

Contact Sign: *see* Pidgin Signed English

Cued Speech: Cued Speech was developed in 1966 by R. Orin Cornett at Gallaudet University in Washington D.C. The cues consist of eight handshapes used in four different positions. These cues are used in combination with the natural mouth movements that occur during speech. Cued Speech helps deaf individuals, while lipreading, to clarify similar sounds.

D

Descriptive name sign: A descriptive name sign is based on one of the person's physical characteristics.

Directional verbs: Directional verbs (also known as "inflecting verbs") are signs that can show "who did what to whom" just by their movement between referents. This movement indicates the subject and the object of the verb in the sentence. For example, if I sign GIVE starting near my body and move it in your direction, then I would be signing the directional verb "me-GIVE-you."

Dominant hand: Your dominant hand is the hand you use to do most of your signing. This is the hand you use for one-handed signs and is the hand that moves when you use a two-handed sign where only one hand is moving.

F

Facial expression: Facial expressions are part of the group of body or face movements called "non-manual markers" and can affect the meaning of signs. While facial expressions only refer to the expressions on your face, non-manual markers refer to facial expressions, head shakes, head nods, head tilts, or any other body movement that can change the meaning of your signs.

Fingerspelling (FS): Fingerspelling is used in ASL to indicate places, names, or ideas for which there is no official sign. It consists of 22 handshapes that represent the 26 letters of the American alphabet when held in certain positions or produced with certain movements.

FS: *see* Fingerspelling

G

Gesture: A gesture is a body movement that is used to communicate.

Gesture Classifiers: These are classifiers where you use your body to act out something. For example, "stomp foot", "give hug", etc.

Glossing: Because ASL is an unwritten language, glossing is a technique used to create a written version of ASL.

Grammar: Grammar is the structure, principles, and rules of a language.

H

Handshape: The handshape of a sign is one of the five parameters of a sign and refers to the shape of the hand, fingers, and palm that is used to form the sign.

I

Iconic signs: Iconic signs are signs that look like the word they are representing. For example, the sign for ELEPHANT is signed like an elephant's trunk.

Idiom: An example of an idiom in English is the phrase "kick the bucket," which means "to die." ASL, however, does not use English idioms. If you were to sign "RAIN CAT DOG" this would actually *mean* cats and dogs are falling from the sky in ASL. So, if you want to sign an English idiom, you need to sign what the idiom actually *means* instead of the exact words. ASL does have its own idioms, though. One idiom would be "TRAIN GONE(CL:G(train)"fade out of sight")" which directly translates into "train go sorry" in English. "Train go sorry," of course, doesn't mean anything in English, but in ASL the sign means, "Sorry, you missed it. I am not going to repeat what I said."

If/then: *see* Conditional sentences

Indexing: Indexing is when you set up a point to refer to a person or object that is or is not present in the signing area. This is also known as referencing or creating referents. If the person or object is present, you can just point at him, her, or it to mean HE/HIM, SHE/HER, or IT. If the person or object is not present, you would first need to identify the person or object. Then, you can "index" the person or object to a point in space. Once you have set up this referent, you can refer back to that same point every time you want to talk about that person or object. To refer to the referents you would use personal pronouns, possessive pronouns, or directional verb signs.

Inflecting verbs: *see* Directional verbs

Inflection: *see* Adverb

Initialized signs: Initialized signs are signs that use the handshape of the first letter of the word. For example, the sign BLUE uses the B handshape.

Instrument Classifiers: These are classifiers where the handshapes show that you are holding something. For example, CL:C(holding cup), CL:S(hold hammer), CL:S(driving), etc.

L

Lexicalized fingerspelling: Lexicalized fingerspelling is fingerspelling that looks more like a sign rather than a fingerspelled word. These are 2-5 letter words that are commonly used and have their own special movements. In glossing, they are indicated by the number (#) symbol. For example, #BACK is a lexicalized sign.

Loan signs: Loan signs are signs that are borrowed from other sign languages. Many loan signs that are borrowed from other countries are the signs that the deaf people in that country use to refer to their country. For example, the American Sign Language sign for CHINA used to be twisting your index finger next to your eye—it referred to the eye shape of Chinese people. That sign is now seen as inappropriate, so ASL has borrowed the sign for CHINA from Chinese Sign Language. We now use the same sign that they use for the word CHINA.

Location: Location is one of the five parameters of a sign and refers to the location of the sign on or in front of your body.

Location Classifiers: These are classifiers where the location of the handshape represents the location of something. For example, CL:5-claw(city here), CL:A(house here), CL:5-claw(bush here), etc.

M

Morpheme: A morpheme is the smallest indivisible unit of syntax that retains meaning. For example, in English, the word "threateningly" consists of four morphemes: "threat," which is a noun; "en," which changes the noun into a verb; "ing," which changes it into an adjective; and "ly" which changes it into an adverb. In ASL, there are no signs for affixes like "en," "ing," "ly," etc. to change the meaning of words. Instead, ASL uses non-manual markers, changes in parameters, and other signs to indicate tense, degree, intensity, plurality, aspect, and more. For example, to explain that someone was walking slowly, you would sign WALK with a slower motion and a facial expression that matches the tone.

Morphology: Morphology is the study of the forms and formations of words.

Movement: Movement is one of the five parameters of a sign and refers to the action that makes the sign.

N

Name signs: Name signs eliminate the need to fingerspell a person's name repeatedly. They are used to identify and refer to people. Usually a Deaf child receives a name sign using the first letter of their name when they attend a residential school. Children with Deaf parents receive a name sign at birth. Hearing people are only given name signs by a Deaf person when they have become involved in the Deaf community.

NMM: *see* Non-manual markers

Non-manual markers (NMM): Non-manual markers are one of the five parameters of a sign and refer to facial expressions and body movements. They can be facial expressions, head shakes, head nods, head tilts, shoulder shrugs, etc. They are used to inflect signs much like vocal intonations are used to inflect spoken words. Inflect means to change, influence, or emphasize the meaning of a sign or signed phrase.

Noun: A noun is a person, place, thing, action, or quality that can act as the subject or object of a sentence.

Noun-verb pairs: In ASL, noun-verb pairs are signs that use the same handshape, location, and orientation, but use a different movement to indicate the difference between the noun and verb. A signed verb usually has a single, continuous movement while a noun usually has a double movement. An example of a noun-verb pair is the sign for CHAIR and the sign for SIT. To sign CHAIR, you would do the motion twice. To sign SIT, you would do the motion once.

Numeral Incorporation: Numeral incorporation means incorporating a number into a sign. For example, instead of signing THREE before the sign WEEK for "three weeks," you would simply use the three-handshape as the handshape for your dominant hand while signing WEEK.

O

Object of a sentence: The object of a sentence is what is involved in the subject's action of the verb. For example, the object of the sentence, "The girl kicked the ball," is "ball."

Object-Subject-Verb (OSV): Object-subject-verb refers to a certain sentence structure used in ASL. An example of this would be the signed sentence, "BALL, GIRL KICK" where the object ("ball") is part of the TOPIC portion of the sentence instead of the COMMENT portion. This is also known as topicalization.

One-handed sign: A one handed sign is a sign that uses only your dominant hand. For example, the sign MAN is a one-handed sign.

Ordinal numbers: Ordinal numbers are the numbers in a series. These are numbers that show the order of something (e.g. first, second, third, etc.)

OSV: *see* Object-Subject-Verb

P

Palm orientation: Palm orientation is one of the five parameters of a sign and refers to the orientation of your palm that is used when making a sign. For example, the sign for YOUR uses the "forward" palm orientation (when your palm is facing away from your body).

Passive voice: Passive voice in a sentence is used to show that the subject is the one "receiving" the action. An example in ASL would be the signed sentence "BALL, GIRL KICK." In English, this is translated into "The ball was kicked by the girl."

Personal pronoun: A personal pronoun is used to refer to the speaker, who the speaker is speaking to, or who the speaker is speaking about. For example, the words "I," "you," "we," "he," "she," "it," and "they" are all personal pronouns. In ASL, personal pronouns are signed by pointing with your index finger toward a person, object, or referent. A referent is used when a person or object is not present.

Phoneme: In spoken languages, like English, a phoneme is a unit of sound that conveys meaning. For example, if you change the "a" in "sad" to "o," you would create "sod," which has a completely different meaning. In ASL, the smallest parts of the language, the phonemes, are handshape, movement, palm orientation, location, and facial expression. For example, if you change the movement of the sign CHAIR to only one movement instead of two, you have just created the sign SIT.

Phonology: Phonology is the study of the smallest part of language that conveys meaning.

Pidgin Signed English (PSE): Pidgin Signed English (also known as "contact signing") is often used when Deaf and hearing people communicate in sign language. It is a "middle ground" between signed English systems and ASL. PSE is not a real language—it just follows English word order while using ASL signs.

Plain verbs: To use a plain verb in ASL, you first need to specify the subject and object of the sentence. For example, the sign CAN is a plain verb. This is unlike directional verbs in ASL, which specify the subject and object of the sentence by its movement alone.

Plural directional verbs: To use a directional verb for something that is being done to multiple people, you would use a sweep, chop, or inward sweep motion. For example, to give a book to a group in general, you would just sweep the sign GIVE, starting near your body, horizontally from your left to your right.

Plural: Plural refers to the form of a word that means there is more than one. In English, the plural form of the word "dog" is "dogs."

Plural Classifiers: These are classifiers where the handshape and movement show that there is more than one of something. For example, (2h)CL:3(cars)"here and here", (2h) CL:4(people in line), etc.

Pluralization: Pluralization means to express something in the plural form. In English, plurals are formed with the "-s" or "-es" suffix. In ASL, you can form a plural by either using repetition, adding a number to the sign, incorporating a number into the sign, using a quantifier sign, using a classifier, repeating the verb, using a sweeping motion, or using reposition.

Possessive pronouns: Possessive pronouns are pronouns that indicate possession. For example, in English, the words "my," "your," "his," "her," "its," "our," and "their" are all possessive pronouns. In ASL, personal pronouns can indicate possession simply by changing the handshape from an index finger to a flat hand. The palm of your flat hand would point toward the person or object. For example, to sign YOUR, you would sign YOU with a flat hand, fingertips up, and your palm facing toward the person you are signing to.

Pragmatics: Pragmatics is the analysis of language in its social context.

Predicate of a sentence: The predicate of a sentence is the part that shows what is being said about the subject. It includes the verb and all the verb's modifiers. For example, in English, the predicate of the sentence, "The girl kicked the ball," would be "kicked the ball."

Prefix: A prefix is an affix that is placed at the beginning of a word. For example, in English, "un-" would be the prefix in the word "unintentional." ASL does not have separate signs for prefixes. You can, however, add an "un-," "im-," or "dis-" prefix to a word by signing the word NOT before it. For example, "NOT BELIEVE" means "disbelieve."

Prepositions: Prepositions show how a noun and a predicate relate. In English, words like "before", "behind", "inside", and "above" are prepositions. Prepositions in ASL are normally shown with classifiers.

Pronoun: A pronoun is a word that takes the place of a noun. In English, words like "she," "it," and "herself" are pronouns. In ASL, pronouns are created by indexing.

PSE: *see* Pidgin Signed English

Punctuation: Punctuation refers to the symbols used in writing to separate sentences, clauses, and phrases to make the meaning clear. In ASL, sentences are normally punctuated by pauses and facial expressions.

Q

Quantifier: In ASL, a quantifier is a separate sign that, when signed with another word, can make the word plural. For example, the signs MANY and FEW are both quantifiers.

Question mark wiggle: A "question mark wiggle" is used to add doubt or incredulousness to a question. You would sign a question mark wiggle by taking your index finger and flexing it a little into almost an x-handshape a few times at the end of a question.

R

Reciprocal Verbs: Directional verbs can also show a reciprocal action, like with the sign (2h)LOOK-AT-EACH-OTHER, where both hands are each directed from a referent and pointing toward each other, representing their eyes looking at each other at the same time.

Referent: In ASL, a referent is when you set up a point to refer to a person or object that is or is not present in the signing area. This is also known as indexing.

Repetition: In ASL, repetition means to repeat a sign. You can use repetition to indicate the tense of a sign or to make a sign plural. For example, you would sign the word CANCEL more than once to mean CANCELLATIONS.

Reposition: In ASL, reposition means to place a sign or classifier in a few places in your signing area to indicate that the word is plural. For example, you can sign HOUSE and then place the classifier used for a house in a few areas in your signing space to mean "A house here, here, and here."

Reversal of orientation: Reversal of orientation is one way to form a negative. When you reverse your palm orientation of some signs, you can express the opposite of the meaning of the original sign. For example, you can change the sign for WANT to don't-WANT by signing WANT then reversing your palm orientation so your palms are facing downward while using a negative facial expression.

Rhetorical question (rhq): Rhetorical questions are not actual questions—a response is not expected. After asking the rhetorical question, you would immediately give the answer and other information. There are certain non-manual markers that are used to create a rhetorical question in ASL. An example of a rhetorical question in ASL would be "ME HUNGRY, WHY? EAT LUNCH NOT" which translates into "I'm hungry because I didn't eat lunch."

Rhq: *see* Rhetorical question

Rochester Method: The Rochester Method is also known as Visible English and focuses on fingerspelling and speech. This method is based on English where each word in a sentence is fingerspelled. This method isn't used much anymore because spelling out each word is a time consuming process.

Role shifting: Role shifting is when you take on the "role" of another person. By doing this, you can show what each person said, did, or felt. Essentially, you can sign a whole story using role shifting. Instead of signing "she said" and then "he said," you can turn your body slightly to the left to sign the comments of one person and then turn your body slightly to the right to sign the comments of the other person. This way, you can "role play" each person.

S

SE: *see* Signed English

Shape Classifiers: These are classifiers where the handshapes trace the exterior shape of something. For example, (2h)CL:B(large box shape), etc.

Sightline: The sightline is the space in the center of the chest. The sightline is significant because focusing on this area enables you to use your peripheral vision to see the signer's hands and face at the same time.

Sign language: Sign language is a manual language expressed by visible hand gestures.

Sign system: In the deaf world, sign systems are types of sign languages that are invented and are not real languages. Sign systems are created for various reasons. For example, Signed English is a sign system and is primarily used for the education of deaf children.

Signed English (SE): Signed English refers to different sign systems that have been developed using borrowed signs from ASL as well as invented signs that represent the words and grammar of English.

Signing space/Signing area: Signing space refers to the pyramid-shaped area on a signer's body where the majority of signs are formed.

Size Classifiers: These are classifiers where the handshape shows the depth or width of something. For example, (2h)CL:C(thick vertical pole), (2h)CL:F(thin vertical pole), (2h)CL:L-curve(small plate), etc.

Spatial verbs: To use a spatial verb in ASL, you first need to specify the subject and object of the sentence. Spatial verbs are used to show moving something "from here to there." Like directional verbs, the movement of the sign is used for the verb. In this case, the movement is to show location—not the subject and object. For example, the sign PUT-up is a spatial verb.

Subject of a sentence: The subject of a sentence is the part that says what the sentence is about. The subject contains the main noun or noun phrase of the sentence. For example, in English, the subject of the sentence, "The girl kicked the ball," would be "girl."

Subject-verb-object (SVO): Subject-verb-object refers to a certain sentence structure used in ASL. An example of this would be the signed sentence, "GIRL KICK BALL" where the subject of the sentence ("girl") is part of the TOPIC portion of the sentence and the object of the sentence ("ball") is part of the COMMENT portion.

Suffix: A suffix is an affix that is placed at the end of a word. For example, in English, "-ly" would be the suffix in the word "slowly." ASL does not have separate signs for suffixes. For example, ASL indicates tense ("-ing," "-ed," and "-s" suffixes) by adding time signs to a sentence.

Surface Classifiers: These are classifiers where the handshape is used to show the surface of something. For example, CL:B(wall), CL:B(hills), etc.

SVO: *see* Subject-verb-object

Syllable: A syllable is how speech sounds are organized in a word. For example, the word "vocabulary" has 5 syllables: "vo-cab-u-lar-y." Each syllable normally consists of one vowel.

Syntax: In ASL, syntax is the order in which signs are placed to form sentences.

T

TC: *see* Total Communication

Temporal Aspect: Temporal aspect means showing how the verb is being done. You can show if something is being done regularly, continually, repeatedly, or for an extended period of time. You would use certain motions (and appropriate facial expressions) to show each.

Tense: Tense refers to inflected forms of verbs that indicate time, such as past, present, or future. In English, words are conjugated, words are added, or suffixes are added to indicate tense. For example, "I went to the store," "Last week I played baseball," or "She noticed him there." In ASL, there is no sign for "went" or for the suffixes "-ing," "-ed," or "-s." Instead, signs like NEXT-WEEK, PAST-MONTH, NOW-AFTERNOON, or NEXT-MONTH are added to signed sentences to indicate tense.

TIME-TOPIC-COMMENT: TIME-TOPIC-COMMENT refers to a certain sentence structure used in ASL. When you talk about a past or future event in ASL, you would establish the time-frame before signing the rest of the sentence. The same rules of word order for the TOPIC-COMMENT structure apply, only now a time-frame is added to the beginning of the sentence. For example, the signed sentence, "YESTERDAY HE WALK" follows this structure.

TOPIC: TOPIC refers to the TOPIC part of the TOPIC-COMMENT sentence structure of ASL syntax. For example, in the ASL sentence, "HOME, ME GO," HOME is the TOPIC.

Topicalization: In ASL, when you use the "object" part of the sentence as the TOPIC of the sentence (OSV word order), this is called topicalization. Certain non-manual markers are necessary in order to sign a topicalized sentence. An example would be the signed sentence, "MY DAD, THAT MAN" which translates into "That man is my dad."

Total Communication (TC): Total Communication is where teachers can use sign, mime, writing, speech, fingerspelling, pictures, or any other educational method that works. The method should depend on the child and the situation. Basically, it is the philosophy that deaf children should be able to learn with whichever method works best for them.

Two-handed non-symmetrical sign: A two-handed non-symmetrical sign uses both your dominant and non-dominant hand where the dominant hand moves while the non-dominant hand remains stationary and sometimes acts as a support base. For example, the sign DRAW is a two-handed non-symmetrical sign.

Two-handed symmetrical sign: A two-handed symmetrical sign uses both your dominant and non-dominant hand where they both move the same way. For example, the sign SCIENCE is a two-handed symmetrical sign.

V

Verb: A verb is a word that is used to represent an action or a state of being and is the essential part of the predicate of a sentence.

Verbal aspect: Verbal aspect refers to the tense of a verb. In ASL, this is produced by changing parameters of the verb. Some changes you can apply include the addition of time signs and repetition.

Verbal number: Verbal number indicates that the action is being done more than once. In ASL, you can only do this with directional verbs. For example, to give a book to a few individuals, you would sign a few short "me-GIVE-you" motions strung together while sweeping your hand horizontally from the left to the right.

Visible English: *see* Rochester Method

W

Whole Classifiers: These are classifiers where the handshape represents a whole object. For example, CL:3(car), CL:1(person), CL:4(people in line), etc.

Whq: *see* Wh-word question

Wh-word question (whq): A wh-word question is a question that requires more than a yes or no answer. These questions normally contain the words "who," "what," "when," "where," "why," or "how." In ASL, certain non-manual markers are required in order to sign a wh-word question.

Word order: Word order refers to the way words are arranged in a sentence.

Y

Y/n: *see* Yes/no question

Yes/no question (y/n): A yes/no question is a question that requires only a yes or no answer. In ASL, certain non-manual markers are required in order to sign a yes/no question.

Resources

If you are interested in studying more in-depth information about ASL grammar, I recommend the following resources:

American Sign Language: A Teacher's Resource on Grammar and Culture, by Charlotte Baker-Shenk and Dennis Cokely

American Sign Language: Student Texts, by Charlotte Baker-Shenk and Dennis Cokely

Learning American Sign Language: Levels I and II, Beginning and Intermediate, by Tom Humphries and Carol Padden

Learning to See: Teaching American Sign Language as a Second Language, by Sherman Wilcox and Phyllis Wilcox

Linguistics of American Sign Language, by Clayton Valli and Ceil Lucas

Index

Rhetorical questions (rhq)
  defined, 144
  glossing, 19, 20,
  syntax, 96
  translation study sheet, 129
Rhq. *See* Rhetorical question
Rochester method, 24–25, 145
Role shifting, 68–69, 78, 124, 145
Roman numerals, 35, 36

S

SE, 23, 24, 145
Sentences, syntax, 89–117. *See also* Individual
Shape classifiers, 77, 145
Shoulder twist, 116
Sightline, 65, 145
Signed English (SE), 23, 24, 145
Signing space, 64–65, 145
Sign systems, 23–25, 50, 145
60's-90's wrist tilt, 41
Size classifiers, 76, 145
Spatial language, 73
Spatial verbs, 79, 145–146
Speed
  classifiers, 73
  inflection, 71, 72
"Sta-sta-sta" mouth movement, 68*t*, 81
"State of being" verbs, 80
States, 32
Stressed signs. *See* Inflection
Subject, of a sentence
  defined, 146
  directional verbs, 110
  word order, 89–93
Subject-verb-object (SVO)
  defined, 146
  topicalization, 99
  word order, 90, 91, 92
Suffixes, 114, 146
Surface classifiers, 76, 146
SVO. *See* Subject-verb-object (SVO)
Syllables, 29, 146
Syntax, 89–117, 146

T

TC, 24, 147
Technology, 55
Temporal aspects, 80–82, 125–126, 146
TEND-TO, 52
Tense
  defined, 146

morphology, 71, 84–85
"state of being verbs," 80
time signs, 82–83
"Thh" mouth movement, 68*t*
"Th" mouth movement, 68*t*
Time
  morphology, 82–87
  translation study sheet, 126
  vocabulary, 41–42
  word order, 93
TIME-TOPIC-COMMENT, 93, 128, 147
Titles, 28
TOPIC, 89, 91, 93, 147
Topicalization (t)
  defined, 147
  glossing, 19
  syntax, 91, 92, 99–100
  translation study sheet, 130–131
TOPIC-COMMENT, 89
Total Communication (TC), 24, 147
"Train go sorry," 55
2h. *See* Two-handed signs
Two-handed signs, 19, 61, 62-63, 147

U

U.S. Supreme Court, 23

V

Variations, common, 55–56
Verbal aspect, 147
Verbs
  auxiliary, 115, 132, 136
  classifiers, 77, 80, 137
  continual, 80, 81
  defined, 147
  directional, 78–79, 92, 102, 110–113, 126–127, 138, 142–143
  indexing, 110–113
  noun pairs, 72–73
  numbers, 147
  plain, 78, 79*p*, 90, 127, 142
  reciprocal, 79, 144
  spatial, 79, 145–146
  temporal aspect, 80–82
  tense, 80, 84–85
  translation study sheet, 125
  types, 78–80
  word order, 89–93
Visible English, 24–25, 145
V handshape, 60
Vocabulary, 27–56

About the Author

Beginning when she was only thirteen years old, Michelle Jay has understood her passion and love for ASL. As a hearing person in the Deaf community, Michelle was determined to master everything she could about ASL… not just "how to sign," but the very best ways to learn to sign as well!

As the founder of **StartASL.com**, the leading online resource for ASL and Deaf Culture, Michelle has tremendous insight into this unique community. Michelle earned a Bachelor's Degree in Deaf Studies, with an emphasis in teaching, from one of the nation's premier programs at California State University, Northridge.

When not writing books or tending her website, Michelle contributes thought-provoking articles to academic publishers such as Greenhaven Press. Her unique articles have done much to support Deaf Culture, and have been printed in resource publications such as *American Chronicle* and *Perspectives on Diseases & Disorders: Deafness & Hearing Impairments*.

Don't Just "Sign"… Communicate!
A Student's Guide to ASL and the Deaf Community

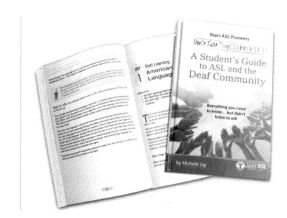

The Heart Of Any Language Is Found Within Its Culture…

As anyone who has learned a foreign language will tell you, all language is an experience. And that experience is found through a language's culture – its people.

The journey toward complete comprehension and usage of American Sign Language includes the recognition, not only of the sovereignty of the language, but of the understanding that ASL lives within its own community and culture.

The full learning and understanding of a language involves much more than vocabulary or sentence structure. All language is unique in vocabulary, grammar, syntax, emotion, and more… including culture. ASL is a language unique to the community that uses it.

Don't Just "Sign"…Communicate! focuses on giving you a better understanding of the ASL community and culture, as well as a better and more comprehensive understanding of learning the language. This guide successfully takes you inside the Deaf community and gets you involved in its fascinating culture.

Take advantage of this informative and handy resource that will make your journey into ASL a fulfilling adventure. Start ASL has created this guide so that you can easily explore the ASL language and Deaf culture. This guide provides you with tools, advice, and helpful resources not available anywhere else!

http://books.startasl.com

CPSIA information can be obtained
at www.ICGtesting.com
Printed in the USA
BVHW090537130920
588369BV00004B/177